Toastin' the Dogs™

Recipes of the Famous and Distinguished

Compiled by Paws With A Cause®

Edited by Lane Phalen, AJ (Candye) Springstead-Sapp,
Kate Thornton and Jennifer Widina

With A PAWS® Dog
Disability Does Not Mean Inability!™

Paws With A Cause® • 1235 - 100th Street SE • Byron Center, MI • 49315
1.800.253.PAWS

Published by Paws With A Cause®
1235 - 100th Street SE
Byron Center, MI 49315
(616) 698-0688
Fax (616) 698-2988
Toll Free 1-800-253-PAWS

ISBN: 0-9643198-0-2
Printed in The United States of America
Cover Art: Imagination Factory
Editors: Lane Phalen, AJ (Candye) Springstead-Sapp,
Kate Thornton and Jennifer Widina

First Printing - Fall 1994

With A PAWS® Dog
Disability Does Not Mean Inability!™

Disability Does Not Mean Inability!™

DEDICATION

This book is dedicated to the many PAWS® Hearing and Service Dog Teams
we have united and to those who will come together in the future.   We
salute their courage and belief in this partnership. A special note of thanks
and appreciation to these very special dogs for their unconditional love and
dedication.

Introduction

Over a year ago when we began working on *Toastin' the Dogs*™, we had no idea what a tremendous response we would get from the "Famous and Distinguished" people who shared their favorite recipes with us. We began to look forward to the mail each day, anticipating the arrival of letters and recipes from Hollywood to Hungary. It is our hope that you are as pleased as we are with the diverse group of people who have graciously agreed to be a part of this cookbook.

One of the goals of this cookbook is to share the PAWS mission with people everywhere. Founded in 1979, today PAWS is the largest producing Hearing and Service Dog provider in the United States. We offer independence, dignity and self esteem to people who are Hearing Impaired/Deaf and Mobility Challenged by training dogs to become their hands, arms, legs and ears. We also provide presentations to the public stressing that people with disabilities are no different than people without disabilities ...things just get done differently.

PAWS Dogs have provided independence to people with a wide scope of disabilities including: Parkinson's, Muscular Dystrophy, Cancer, Epilepsy, Spina Bifida, Spinal Cord Injuries, Deafness, Hearing Impairment and Cerebral Palsy. We remain committed to providing people with disabilities a Hearing or Service Dog that is trained specifically for their needs. Each PAWS Dog's training is tailored to each recipients requirements. As the person's needs change, so does the training of his or her dog. When a person with a disability receives a PAWS Dog, they also receive a support network of Field Representatives throughout the United States to assist them throughout the lifetime of the Team.

An additional goal of this cookbook is to raise funds so that we can continue our efforts. We are very proud of the fact that over 90% of all monies spent by PAWS over the past four years went directly into program services. All of the profits from the sale of *Toastin' the Dogs*™ will be used to help PAWS continue to provide services that INSPIRE and ENCOURAGE people with disabilities to attain the DIGNITY of INDEPENDENCE.

We have done our best to accurately reproduce the recipes submitted to PAWS® and encourage you to try all of them.

Thank you for your purchase and enjoy!

TABLE OF CONTENTS

Table of Contents

Table of Contents

Table of Contents

Table of Contents

Table of Contents

Table of Contents

If you are looking for a special dish,

you can reference our Recipe Index located at the back of the book.

Enjoy These
Dog-Gone
Delicious Dishes!

Fannie Abzug's
CHEESE CAKE RECIPE
Bella S. Abzug
Lawyer/Activist

1 1/2 pounds of pot cheese
1/4 pound of cream cheese
6 eggs
1 teaspoon vanilla
2 tablespoons corn starch
1/2 cup of butter or margarine
1/2 pint of sour cream or yogurt
1 cup of sugar or sweetener (can be less)

Strain the cheese twice through a colander using the bottom of a glass. Add egg yolks, vanilla, corn starch, butter, sour cream, and sugar. Beat egg whites until stiff and fold into the above ingredients. Put in a spring form. Bake in a slow oven about 300° for one hour. Let cool in oven with door closed.

DON'T LOOK.

Base   *Graham crackers for pie crust*

Dissolve graham crackers like a cereal base. Mix with butter and sugar. (A ready made graham cracker pie crust can be purchased at a super market.)

Enjoy!

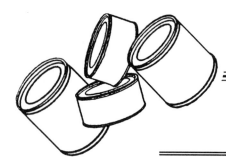

"TYPICAL ADAMS LUNCH"
Bryan Adams
Musician

1 *can Heinz baked beans*

2 *slices of toast (fairly brown) with butter*

Heat beans for approximately 3-5 minutes. While beans are heating, toast the bread and then butter it.

Place hot steaming beans on the toast then serve!!

Preparation time: next to nothing.

Crab *Cindy*
Gossip Reporter of *The New York Post*
Cindy Adams

1 1/2 cups dry noodles
1 can (10 1/2 ounces) cream of shrimp soup
1/2 cup each milk, mayonnaise, & sharp cheddar cheese grated
frozen onion rings
8 ounces each of fresh crab and fresh shrimp

Mix all ingredients except onion rings thoroughly. Cover and refrigerate overnight. Bake at 350° for 30 minutes. Uncover and place desired amount of frozen onion rings on top. Bake, uncovered, for another 15 minutes.

KOREAN CHICKEN
Daniel K. Akaka
U.S. Senator - Hawaii

5 pound bag of chicken

Batter: 1/2 - 1 cup flour
1 tablespoon salt

Sauce: 1 stalk green onion
1/2 cup shoyu
6 tablespoons sugar
1 clove garlic, chopped
1 teaspoon sesame oil
1 small red pepper (optional)

Salt chicken and let stand overnight. Roll chicken in flour and fry. After frying, dip in sauce and serve.

Daniel K Akaka

CROWN ROAST OF PORK
John R. Albers, Chairman and CEO
Dr. Pepper/Seven-Up Companies, Inc.

"I have literally prepared these in my home kitchen."

1 crown roast of pork

Have crown made by butcher from 8 strips of pork loin, about 20 ribs [6-8 pound]. For easy carving and shaping, backbone is always removed.

1 package curly endive
heavy duty foil
red crab apples

Season with salt and pepper. Place in roasting pan on a rack, if possible, done ends up. Wrap bone ends in aluminum foil to prevent excessive browning. Roast, uncovered, in 325° oven for 20 to 25 minutes per pound of meat, 2 1/2 to 3 1/2 hours. Use meat thermometer if you have one. One hour before the meat is done, place double layer of heavy duty foil between the roast and rack and return roast and rack to roasting pan. Fill center of roast with mushroom stuffing, about 2 quarts. Put extra stuffing around the roast or in a casserole. The latter is neater. Return to oven for last hour of roasting.

To serve, use a large tray surrounded with curly endive and place roast in the middle. Replace foil wraps on the bone ends with red crab apples on every other bone. Put remaining crab apples around roast on endive. Take roast to the table and have Host carve one rib per serving. Host will also give each guest a spoon of stuffing. This roast makes an impressive sight, so be sure not to carve before all are seated.

(More...)

the MUSHROOM STUFFING

1 1/2 sticks butter
1/2 cup finely minced onion
8 cups (2 quarts fine bread crumbs)
(or 1 large loaf sliced bread cubed)
1/2 cup chicken stock
1 pound fresh mushrooms, washed & sliced

1/2 teaspoon pepper
1/2 teaspoon dried sage
1 small can water chestnuts
1 cup chopped celery
2 teaspoons salt

Melt butter in large heavy skillet or Dutch oven. Add onion, cook 3 minutes. Stir in bread. Heat, stirring to prevent excessive browning. Turn into deep bowl. Mix remaining ingredients. Mix in broth a little at a time, to moisten crumbs. Cool, place in middle of crown roast. Garnish with sliced water chestnuts. Bake 1 hour.

CAULIFLOWER/GREEN PEA PLATTER

1 large head of cauliflower
¾ cups water
¼ teaspoon salt
dash of pepper
2 packages of frozen peas
salt, pepper, butter to taste
Mustard Sauce
chopped chives

Mustard Sauce
1 cup sour cream (room temperature)
1 tablespoon lemon juice
2 tablespoons prepared mustard
¼ teaspoon salt

Place whole cauliflower in a pan and add the water. Season with salt and pepper. Cover and bring to boil over medium heat and cook for about 15 minutes or until tender, but crisp. In another pan, cook peas according to package directions. Season to taste with salt, pepper and a couple of tablespoons of butter. Just before serving, place hot cooked cauliflower in center of platter and arrange hot cooked peas around it. Cover cauliflower with mustard sauce and sprinkle with chopped chives.

Mustard Sauce: combine ingredients.

GRANDMA'S APPLE PIE
Harry Anderson
Actor and Magician

Peel, core and thinly slice 6 big Red Delicious Apples. Slice apple quarters into thirds or quarters. Toss with 1 cup of sugar, 1 teaspoon of cinnamon and 2 tablespoons of flour. Let this sit while you make the pastry.

Mix 2 cups of unbleached white flour and 1 teaspoon salt. Cut in ¼ cup butter, ½ cup shortening until it resembles cornmeal. Add 5-6 tablespoons of ice water. Sometimes I use one teaspoon of vinegar in this too. Lightly blend and gather dough into a ball. Roll out bottom crust and put in pan. Roll out top crust, put apples in pan including all liquid, dot with butter and sprinkle with one tablespoon of water, place top crust on and seal. Cut slits.

Bake at 375° for one hour. It will boil over so bake it on a cookie sheet.

COTTAGE CHEESE MEATLOAF
JULIE ANDREWS
Actress/Singer

1 pound lean ground beef
      or ground veal
1/2 cup quick-cooking rolled oats
1 tablespoon prepared mustard
3/4 teaspoon salt
1/3 cup grated Parmesan cheese

1 cup (1/2 pint) cottage cheese
1 egg
1/4 cup ketchup
2 tablespoons chopped onion
1/8 teaspoon pepper

Combine the ground meat with the cottage cheese, egg, rolled oats, ketchup, mustard, onion, salt and pepper. Mix all ingredients lightly until well blended.

Press the mixture loosely into a shallow baking pan (about 8 inches square).

Bake, uncovered, in a 350° oven for 20 minutes. Remove from oven and sprinkle the Parmesan cheese evenly over the top. Return to the oven and continue to bake for 10 minutes.

Let stand for 5 minutes before cutting into squares. Double the quantity and put one loaf in freezer.

PHEASANT PIE
Cecil D. Andrus
Governor of Idaho

1 pheasant, 3 to 4 pounds dressed weight

1 bay leaf	*1/8 teaspoon pepper*
1 stalk celery	*1/4 teaspoon salt*
6 peppercorns	*1 1-pound can pearl onions*
1 tablespoon salt	*1 14-ounce can sliced mushrooms*
1/2 cup butter	*(optional)*
1/2 cup flour	*1 package frozen peas*
1 cup light cream	*2 canned pimentos, sliced*
	1 box pastry mix

Place pheasant in large kettle and cover with water. Add bay leaf, celery, peppercorn, and 1 tablespoon salt. Bring to a boil. Cover and cook over low heat 2 to 3 hours, or until pheasant is tender. (Can be done the day before.) Remove meat from bones; strain broth. Melt butter in saucepan; add flour and stir until blended. Gradually add 2 cups of the broth, stirring constantly. Add light cream, pepper, and salt. Cook, stirring constantly. Add light cream, pepper, and salt. Cook, stirring until thickened. Arrange pheasant pieces, onions, mushrooms, peas, and pimentos in 2-quart casserole. Add sauce, leaving at least 1 inch space at top.

Prepare pastry mix. Cut pastry circle 1/2 inch larger than casserole and place over pheasant mixture, turning edge of pastry under and pressing to casserole with fork or spoon. Bake in preheated 450° oven until crust is golden brown - 15 to 30 minutes or longer if necessary. *Makes 4 to 6 servings.*

---

the PERFECT IDAHO®
BAKED POTATO

Scrub Idaho® potatoes well. Dry potatoes and prick with a fork. Bake in a 425° oven for 55 to 65 minutes, until soft. Or, bake potatoes in a 350° oven for one hour and 25 minutes or one hour and 30 minutes. Serve immediately with seasoned butter, sour cream, or your favorite cheese sauce.

IDAHO® POTATO
CASSEROLE

3 lbs. of frozen Idaho® hash brown potatoes (thawed)
2 cans cream of mushroom soup
½ cup evaporated milk
2 tablespoons plain milk
½ cup chopped onion
½ cup butter, melted
1 pint sour cream
1 cup grated cheese

Mix all together and stir in potatoes. Top with more grated cheese and Ritz cracker crumbs. Bake at 350° for 30 to 40 minutes. This recipe freezes well.

BALSAMIC ROASTED NEW POTATOES
Edward Asner
Actor/Activist

2 tablespoons olive oil
2 pound small new potatoes, washed,
patted dry, quartered
1 tablespoon minced garlic
1 tablespoon minced shallot
1 teaspoon fresh thyme
1 teaspoon minced rosemary
1/8 teaspoon freshly ground nutmeg
1/4 cup balsamic vinegar
salt, pepper

Heat olive oil in a 12" skillet over medium-high heat. Add potatoes, garlic and shallot. Toss in skillet until well mixed. Add thyme, rosemary and nutmeg. Toss well again. When potatoes are hot, transfer to baking sheet and spread in single layer. (Can be made several hours ahead to this point.)

Place sheet on rack in lower third of 400° oven. Roast potatoes until golden and just tender, about 25 minutes, turning once midway. Add vinegar. Toss well. Season to taste with salt and pepper. Return to oven until sizzling, about 7 minutes. Serve immediately. Makes 6 servings.

"It's a wonderful, low fat dish that goes with anything."

MOTHER TAEUSCH'S PECAN TARTS
Michael Avallone
Author

*a.k.a. "Mark Dane, Steve Michaels, Nick Carter,
Troy Conway, Edwina Noone, Priscilla Dalton,
Dorothea Nile, Sidney Stuart, Jean-Anne De Pre,
Dora Highland, Amanda Jean-Jarrett,
Lee Davis Willoughby, Ed Noon, Memo Morgan,
Fred Frazer, James Blaine. Stuart Jason, Vance Stanton
& some very famous ghosts never to be mentioned."*

1 package (3 ounces) cream cheese, softened
1/2 cup butter or margarine, softened
3/4 cup brown sugar, firmly packed
1 tablespoon butter (or margarine), softened
1 teaspoon pecan flavor (or vanilla flavor)
1 cup sifted flour
dash of salt
1 egg
2/3 cup chopped pecans, divided

*C*ombine cream cheese, 1/2 cup butter, and flour in medium size mixing bowl. Chill, covered for 1 hour. Shape into 24 one-inch balls. Press each dough ball over bottom and up sides of ungreased miniature muffin pans.

Preheat oven to 325º. Combine egg, brown sugar, pecan flavor, salt, and 1 tablespoon butter in small mixing bowl. Beat until smooth. Divide 1/3 cup pecans among tarts. Pour egg mixture into muffin cups. Top with remaining 1/3 cup pecans.

*B*ake 25 minutes or until lightly browned. Cool slightly. Remove from pan with fork. Makes 24 tarts.

Heart Smart Hot as Hades
Spicy Shrimp
Nancy Banaitis
Food Editor, Cosmopolitan Home Magazine
Private Chef Jay Van Andel Family

1 pound large shrimp unpeeled and uncooked. Wash and pat dry
2 stalks green onion - cut crosswise, in large slices
2 tablespoon favorite Cajun seasoning - more or less, you decide
1 large pepper - green, red, or yellow
each or combined, sliced thick lengthwise

"If you want this to have an Oriental flavor,
use any favorite Oriental hot sauce."

2 cloves garlic - diced fine
1 can stewed tomatoes (drain well), **or**
3 fresh tomatoes peeled and seeded
1 medium Bermuda onion
peel, trim ends carefully, preserving the roundness of the onion.

From top to bottom, slice downward, cutting into the onion, creating two halves. Then laying one cut end flat to the surface of your cutting board, slice thin slices, lengthwise, into the onion. Repeat on other half.

"Practice shuffling the pan on the range top.
It is done by sliding the pan back and forth with quick sharp
strokes. It is usually done to impress bystanders
with your skill and professional ease in the kitchen."

You will be sautéing in a non-stick pan that has been sprayed with garlic or vegetable non-stick spray. Heat pan on medium high to get it nice and hot, when it is, spray with non-stick spray. Add shrimp, green onion, large pepper, then season with the Cajun spice. Working quickly, *wrestle it around with your professional pan shuffle,* or a wooden spoon, so that all sides get seasoned and cooked. Reach into tomato can, and squeeze any more of the juice from the tomato with your hand, in the can. With a theatrical flair, crush the tomato between your fingers as you spread it over the shrimp. Add the sliced onions, and slide onto serving plate. If serving cold, wrap with plastic wrap and chill.

INDIANA MINT BROWNIES
Evan Bayh
Governor of Indiana

1 cup all-purpose flour
1 cup sugar
1 16-ounce can chocolate-flavored syrup (1 1/2 cups)
4 eggs
1/2 cup butter or margarine, softened
Mint Cream (recipe follows)
Chocolate Topping (recipe follows)

In a mixing bowl, beat together the flour, sugar, syrup, eggs, and butter or margarine with an electric mixer on low speed till combined, then 1 minute on medium speed. Turn mixture into a greased 13x9x2 baking pan. Bake in a 350° oven for 30 to 35 minutes or until top springs back when lightly touched. Top may still appear wet. Let cook in pan on wire rack.

Meanwhile, prepare Mint Cream and Chocolate Topping. Allow Chocolate Topping to cool 10 to 15 minutes before spreading on cooled brownies. Spread Mint Cream over the cooled brownies. Pour slightly cooled Chocolate Topping over mint layer. Cover and chill for at least 1 hour. Store the brownies in the refrigerator. Makes about 50 small brownies.

MINT CREAM

In a small mixing bowl, beat together 2 cups sifted powdered sugar, 1/2 cup softened butter or margarine, 1 tablespoon water, 1/2 teaspoon mint extract, and 3 drops green food coloring, if you like. Beat till smooth.

CHOCOLATE TOPPING

In a heavy, small saucepan, combine 1 cup semi-sweet mint-flavored chocolate pieces or semi-sweet chocolate pieces, and 6 tablespoons butter or margarine. Cook over low heat till chocolate melts. *Or,* in a small microwave-safe bowl, microcook on 100% power (high) for 1 to 1 1/2 minutes or till chocolate melts, stirring occasionally.

SWEET AND SOUR CHICKEN
Robert F. Bennett
United States Senator - Utah

"...my two favorite recipes ... tasty and kind to the waste-line. Regrettably, I do not know a good recipe for doggie bones."

1 1/2 pounds chicken breasts cut in strips
1 #2 can pineapple chunks (2 1/2 cup size) including juice
1/4 cup brown sugar

2 tablespoons cornstarch	1/2 teaspoon salt
1/2 cup water	1/4 cup green onions, sliced
1/4 cup vinegar	1 small green pepper, cut in strips
1 tablespoon soy sauce	1 small red pepper, cut in strips

Brown chicken in hot skillet sprayed with *Pam*; add water. Cover and simmer until done (about 10 minutes). Set aside. Combine brown sugar, cornstarch, pineapple juice, vinegar, soy sauce, and salt in saucepan. Cook and stir over medium heat until thick. Pour over hot chicken, (may refrigerate at this point) and let stand for 10 minutes. Add raw green and red peppers, onion, and pineapple. Cook 2 to 3 minute. Serve over rice. Serves 6 to 8 people.

LIGHT STRAWBERRY CAKE

1 box light white cake mix
16 ounces frozen unsweetened strawberries, thawed, mashed and drained
(reserve 2 tablespoons liquid)
1/2 cup water
3 egg whites
1 teaspoon strawberry extract
1/2 cup powdered sugar

Preheat oven to 350º. Spray a 9 x 13 inch glass baking dish with non-stick vegetable coating. Place cake mix in a large mixing bowl and add strawberries, water, egg whites and extract. Blend on low speed for 30 seconds. Beat on medium 2 minutes, scraping sides of bowl with rubber spatula. Pour into prepared pan. Bake 30 minutes, until top springs back when touched lightly. Combine reserved strawberry liquid with powdered sugar and pour evenly over warm cake. Makes 12 servings.

BROCCOLI BLUE CHEESE FETTUCINE
Brian Boitano
Olympic Figure Skater

1 bunch broccoli, tough stems removed,
        broken into small flowerettes
1 stick butter
4 large garlic cloves, chopped
2 large whole green onions finely chopped
1/2 cup heavy or whipping cream
1/4 pound blue cheese, crumbled
1/4 cup freshly grated Parmesan cheese
3/4 pound fresh fettucine
salt
lots of freshly ground pepper

Steam broccoli until just tender, then chop. You should have about 2 1/4 cups. Melt butter in a large skillet. Add garlic, green onion, and broccoli; sauté for three minutes. Stir in cream, salt, and pepper, and cook at a gentle boil until sauce thickens slightly. Toss sauce with hot pasta in a serving bowl. Add blue cheese and toss to distribute evenly. Add *Parmesan* cheese and toss again. Serve immediately, with extra grated cheese and pepper on the side. Serves 4.

FRUIT SPICE SQUARES
Rt. Hon. J.B. Bolger
Prime Minister of New Zealand

5 ounces butter
1 cup sugar
2 cups flour
1 teaspoon baking powder
2 tablespoons milk

Cream butter and sugar, add remaining ingredients. Divide the mixture in half. Press half into sponge roll tin and cover with the following filling:

8 ounces sultanes
1/2 cup sugar
1/2 cup water
1 large teaspoon flour
1 large teaspoon butter
1 teaspoon cinnamon
1 teaspoon mixed spice
1 teaspoon cocoa

Combine all together in saucepan and bring to the boil. Spread over base in tin and crumble remainder of first mixture on top. Bake at 350° for approximately 30 minutes.

TACO SALAD
Erma Bombeck
Syndicated Columnist and Author

1 head lettuce, finely chopped
1/2 pound ground sirloin of beef
2 large tomatoes, diced
1 1/2 cups grated cheddar cheese
3/4 cup your own favorite dressing
3 tablespoons sour cream

Wash and chop lettuce in advance. Place lettuce in a colander so that all moisture can drip out of the lettuce before preparing the salad. Place colander in the refrigerator. Crumble the ground sirloin and cook over medium heat until just done.

Put the chopped lettuce, diced tomatoes, cooked warm sirloin, and 3/4 cup of the grated cheddar cheese in a large mixing bowl. Add your favorite dressing and toss well. Divide the salad on 6 plates. Sprinkle remaining 3/4 cup of grated cheddar cheese evenly on top of each serving. Put 1 1/2 teaspoons sour cream on top of each salad. I like to serve this with Toasted Tortilla Triangles. Makes 6 servings.

MISSOURI APPLE SOUP
Christopher S. Bond
U.S. Senator, Missouri

"Stephenson's Apple Orchard in eastern Jackson County is a name that brings to mind family outings during the fall picking season and bushel baskets heaping with succulent apples. Why not reserve a few Jonathans for this unusual soup?"

2 tablespoons butter
2 medium onions, thinly sliced
6 Red Jonathan apples, peeled, cored, and diced
4 cups chicken broth
2 tablespoons sugar
1 tablespoon curry powder, or to taste
salt and freshly ground white
pepper to taste
1-2 cups light cream, to taste

In *a Dutch oven,* melt butter, sauté onions until transparent. Add apples, broth, sugar, and curry powder. Season with salt and pepper. Cook covered over low heat until apples are soft.

Strain apples and onions from broth and reserve, set broth aside. Place apples and onions in a food processor or blender, puree. Add broth, blend well. Add cream according to desired richness, chill. Taste and adjust seasoning. Garnish with thin apple wedges and a sprinkling of sliced almonds. 10 to 12 servings.

ROCK CORNISH HENS
Victor Borge
Musician/Comedian

6 Rock Cornish pullets
1/4 pound butter
1 1/4 cups water
Salt and pepper
1 tablespoon water (or more to make paste)
3 teaspoons flour
1/2 cup light cream
Sauce coloring
1/2 teaspoon sugar

Rub the insides of the pullets with salt and pepper. Sear in butter in a Dutch oven until golden brown--ten to twelve minutes.

"If a clock is not available,
play the 'Minute Waltz' ten to twelve times."

Add water and let simmer, covered, until tender-- approximately thirty-five minutes. Remove birds; prepare sauce: stir like crazy into drippings a paste of cold water and three teaspoons flour. Stir in cream, salt, tasteless coloring and sugar. Pour sauce over pullets and serve. Serves six.

New Jersey BLUEBERRY or CRANBERRY MUFFINS
Bill Bradley *and his wife* Ernestine
U.S. Senator, New Jersey

*Nationally, New Jersey ranks second and third respectively
in the production
of blueberries and cranberries.*

2 cups sifted flour (unbleached)
1/2 cups sugar
2 1/2 teaspoons baking powder
3/4 teaspoon salt
1 well-beaten egg
1 cup milk
1/3 cup salad oil
1 cup fresh or thawed and well drained
   blueberries or cranberries

Sift dry ingredients into bowl; make a well in the center.

Combine egg, milk, and oil. Add all at once to dry ingredients. Stir *quickly*, just until dry ingredients are blended. *Gently* stir in blueberries or cranberries. Fill greased muffin pan 2/3 full. Bake at 400° for about 25 minutes. Makes 12 muffins.

Bill Bradley

IOWA APPLESAUCE CAKE
Terry E. Branstad
Governor, Iowa

1/2 cup butter, margarine, or shortening
3/4 cup sugar
3/4 cup packed brown sugar
1 egg
2 cups all-purpose flour
2 teaspoons baking powder
1 teaspoon baking soda
1 teaspoon ground cinnamon
1/2 teaspoon ground cloves
1 1/2 cups applesauce
1 cup raisins
1/2 cup chopped walnuts or pecans

*I*n a large mixing bowl, beat the butter, margarine, or shortening for 30 seconds. Add the sugars and egg; beat until combined.

Stir together the flour, baking powder, baking soda, and spices. Add flour mixture alternately with applesauce to butter mixture.

Stir in raisins and nuts. Pour batter into a greased 13x9x2 inch baking pan, spreading evenly. Bake in a 350° oven for 30-35 minutes, or until a toothpick inserted near the center comes out clean. Cool in pan on wire rack. Serves 12.

CREAM CHEESE FROSTING

Beat together 2 3-ounce packages softened cream cheese, 1 1/2 cup softened butter (or margarine) and 2 teaspoons vanilla until light and fluffy. Gradually beat in 2 cups sifted powdered sugar. Beat in 2 1/2 to 2 3/4 cups sifted powdered sugar to make a spreadable frosting. A butter frosting could be used instead of the cream cheese.

For a decorative finish, set a doily lightly on the frosted cake and sprinkle lightly with a mixture of cinnamon and nutmeg. Carefully remove the doily.

CAROL'S CREOLE BLACK BEANS
Carol Moseley Braun
U.S. Senator, Illinois

3 cups cooked black beans (Goya canned or homemade)
1 1/2 large onions
1 large green pepper
3/4 teaspoon garlic
1/4 teaspoon cumin (ground)
8 ounces olive oil (extra virgin)
1 teaspoon vinegar
bacon

Sausage: Andouille or Tasso is preferred, but in a pinch, Italian sausage will do.

Beans: A real gourmet will start from scratch, cook black beans with ham bone.

Sauté green pepper in bacon fat; then add onion and let brown slowly. Add garlic; sauté. Add beans, olive oil, and cumin.

Add meat (cooked); simmer at low heat. Add vinegar for about 5 minutes. Mash beans to achieve thickness.

It always tastes better if let settle overnight. You may add other meats such as ham, pork, smoked meat, or even smoked turkey.

Carol Moseley Braun

CAJUN DEEP FRIED TURKEY
John Breaux
U.S. Senator, Louisiana

4 ounces liquid garlic
4 ounces liquid onion
4 ounces liquid celery
1 tablespoon red pepper
2 tablespoons salt
2 tablespoons Tabasco
1 ounce liquid crab boil, **or**
1 tablespoon Old Bay Seasoning

1 poultry or meat injector
1 defrosted 10-12 pound turkey
5 gallons peanut oil

Sauté first 7 ingredients until salt and pepper are dissolved. Fill injector and inject turkey at breast, wings, drumsticks, thighs, and back. Allow to marinate 24 hours in refrigerator or ice chest. Use a 10 gallon pot for frying. Bring peanut oil to 350° temperature and fry turkey for 38-42 minutes. Turkey should float to surface after 35 minutes and you should cook an additional 5-7 minutes. You may want to tie turkey legs with 1/2" cotton ropes to be removed when done.

Cooking of fried turkey should be done outdoors. Extreme caution should be taken when placing cold turkey into hot oil.

Grandma Daigle's RICE DRESSING MIX

1 pound ground meat
3 tablespoons cooking oil
1 cup chopped onion
1 cup chopped celery
1 large chopped bell pepper
3 cups cooked rice

1/2 cup chopped green onion tops
1/2 cup chopped parsley
salt and pepper to taste
1 cup water
2 tablespoons Kitchen Bouquet
(optional)

Cook meat in oil in large pot until brown. Add onions, celery, bell pepper. Reduce heat and cook until wilted. Add water and all other ingredients, except rice. Simmer for about 45 minutes. Add more water if needed to keep about the same amount of juice started with. Add to cooked rice and keep warm until ready to serve. Serves 10 to 12.

(More...)

1 pint of heavy cream (or half & half)
1/2 pound of Tasso
3 pounds of shrimp
1/2 teaspoon of thyme
3/4 teaspoon salt
1/2 cup chopped green onions
1/4 teaspoon black pepper
1/2 cup chopped parsley
1/4 teaspoon white pepper
1 or 2 packs of fresh
1/4 teaspoon red pepper
1/2 teaspoon sweet basil
Angel Hair fettucini

*B*ring cream to a boil and add tasso and seasonings and reduce heat and let simmer for 10 to 15 minutes. Add 3 pounds shrimp and cook for 5 minutes over medium heat. Add chopped green onions and parsley. Add fresh fettucini and cook for 3 minutes.   Serves 6 people.

John Breaux

MEATBALLS
Hank Brown
U.S. Senate, Colorado

1 pound hamburger
1 large diced onion
2 tablespoons flour
salt and pepper

Mix with fork and fingers, roll into balls, a little larger than golf balls -- brown over slow heat, turning often.

Add 1 can (pound) tomatoes (strain pulp of tomatoes through a strainer). Simmer at least 1 full hour.

Serve over mashed potatoes.

Hank Brown

Applesauce for Dessert
Helen Gurley Brown, Editor
COSMOPOLITAN

For each person use:

1 good apple, cored and cut into about 20 pieces -- leaving the skin on; and 1 or 2 pieces lemon peel.

Put in heavy pot with a lid, cook on lowest flame possible until apples get mushy -- ten or fifteen minutes. (Can be done with higher heat if in a hurry.)

When apples are mushy, mash to a pulp (lemon peel can be left in for more flavor) with potato masher, add one packet Equal or Sweet 'N Low.

While still warm, put in crystal dessert dish and top with 1/2 carton plain yogurt sweetened with 1 packet Equal or Sweet 'N Low. Dust nutmeg on top.

Total calories: 158. Calorie count can be cut by not using this much yogurt or even this much applesauce.

Apple-- 80 calories
Yogurt-- 70 calories
Sweetener-- 8 calories
158 calories

SUPPLY-SIDE FUDGE
William F. Buckley, Jr.
Originally published in National Review in 1981

Dear Mrs. Wells:

I had a most engaging letter from Barnaby Conrad (III), the gist of which is that I must give you a recipe for your new book. I have been reluctant to do so not so much from any fear for my reputation, but for yours, since no red-blooded American would buy a book including a recipe by me without demanding his money back. The fact of it is that I am 55 years old, that I cooked feverishly during two summers, age 14 and 15, that I made a considerable sum of money from my cooking-- something on the order of $24 or $25 per summer. I produced a most delicious fudge, which I sold via an old ladies' institution in Sharon, Connecticut at 65 cents per pound (with nuts, 75 cents). My father was so unkind as to point out, somewhere along the line, that the economic model after which I had fashioned my enterprise was unrealistic inasmuch as I used exclusively ingredients provided gratis by my father's kitchen.

Anyway (for a double portion):

1 1/2 cups of milk
4 squares of Baker's chocolate
1/2 pound of butter
2 cups of sugar

Stir until you see what looks like discrete goblets. Test these by dripping, by teaspoon, a drop or two. If they come down fragmented, you must leave the mixture under boil. If they come down whole, you are ready to lift the mess off the stove. (On no account should you pass by stage two from inattention, because the effect of this is a granular fudge.)

At this moment, you should add a teaspoon of salt and, a minute or two later, two to three teaspoons of vanilla extract. The point of waiting this long is that you must not allow the vanilla to evaporate. If you are living in the post-industrial revolution you may submit the whole to a blender, adding nuts or not, according to market demands, always assuming you are not a supply-sider; in which case you should add the nuts malgre soi. The beating should continue until the stuff is very nearly cool, and only then pour it into a plate.

Beyond that, I know only how to make a stew composed of ingredients from the Democratic platform, but that would be coprophagous.

Yours faithfully,
Wm. F. Buckley Jr.

HURRY CURRY SAUCE
Dale Bumpers
U.S. Senator, Arkansas

3 egg yolks
2 tablespoons light cream or milk
1 to 2 tablespoons freshly squeezed lemon juice
1/2 teaspoon curry powder
salt to taste
1/4 teaspoon butter or margarine, melted

IN the container of electric blender or food processor, combine egg yolks, cream, lemon juice, curry powder, and salt. Process 10 seconds or until sauce is smooth and slightly thickened. With blender on low speed, gradually pour in melted butter while it is still bubbly hot. Process 10 seconds or until sauce is smooth and slightly thickened. Serve sparingly over vegetables such as cauliflower, broccoli, and asparagus or over poached eggs.

BARBI'S SPINACH DIP AND BREAD

1 pound round pumpernickel bread
2 cups sour cream
2 cups Hellman's mayonnaise
1 small onion chopped
2 packages Knorr vegetable soup mix
2 packages frozen chopped spinach--squeeze out water

Mix 2 hours before serving, chill. Immediately before serving hollow out bread, and fill hollow with dip. You may toast the bread and use as dipsters. Also one can of sliced water chestnuts can be added to dip.

SNICKER DOODLE COOKIES

Sift together 2 3/4 cups flour, 2 teaspoons cream of tartar, 1 teaspoon of soda, 1/2 teaspoon of salt. Combine 1 cup (2 sticks) margarine, 1 1/2 cups sugar, 2 eggs beaten until creamy. Add the dry ingredients, mix thoroughly, chill 2 hours. Roll teaspoons of dough in mixture of 2 tablespoons sugar, 1 teaspoon cinnamon. Place 2 inches apart on ungreased cookie sheet. Bake in 400° oven 8 to 10 minutes.

CHICKEN DIVAN
Chris Burke
Actor

4 whole chicken breasts
3 packages frozen broccoli spears
2 cans cream of chicken soup
3/4 cup mayonnaise
1 teaspoon lemon juice
1/2 teaspoon curry powder
2 tablespoon melted butter
3/4 cup shredded cheddar cheese
1/2 cup bread crumbs

Boil breasts for 1/2 hour, skin and slice.

Cook spears according to package directions.

Place on bottom of serving dish. Use butter to grease dish (1 tablespoon).

Cover with chicken slices.

Mix soup, mayo, juice, curry.

Pour over chicken.

Mix 1 tablespoon butter and crumbs and spread over top.

Bake at 350° for 40 minutes.

Serves 6-8.

Ground Beef Jerky
Conrad Burns
U.S. Senator, Montana

"The following recipe has been in my wife's family for years and is a favorite of mine."

1 pound ground beef
2 teaspoons salt
1/4 teaspoon pepper
1 teaspoon chili powder
1 teaspoon garlic powder
1 teaspoon onion powder
1/4 teaspoon ginger
1 teaspoon smoke liquid

Blend the spices well into the meat. Divide into two portions. Lay this meat mixture between two pieces of plastic. Using a rolling pin, roll to 1/4" thickness. Remove top layer of paper. Turn a cake cooling rack over the meat mixture and invert. Peel off the other layer of plastic.

Place in the middle shelf of oven and dry at about 175° for approximately 6 hours. You may want to place some aluminum foil on the shelf below to catch the drippings. Leave the oven door open 2-3". When done, cut into 1" strips with shears.

BARLEY CASSEROLE
Leo Buscaglia
Author

"I love good food! I love to eat. I love to share. And when you find a dish that's so good, so inexpensive and so healthful, it should be offered to everyone!"

1/2 cup butter
1 onion, chopped
1 cup mushrooms, chopped
1 cup barley
4 cups bouillon
(chicken, beef or vegetable)
seasoning to taste

In a sauce pan, melt butter and sauté onion and mushrooms until tender. Do not overcook. Place barley in large casserole, add the above cooked ingredients and sauté about two minutes. Pour in bouillon and stir. Cover casserole and place in oven at 350° for 1 hour and 15 minutes or until liquid is absorbed and barley is al dente.

"THEN, prepare for exclamations of approval when served!"

CHILE RELLENO CASSEROLE
Ben Nighthorse Campbell
U. S. Senator, Colorado

"This recipe is ideal for buffet-style gatherings where you would like to serve rellenos for many, without the trouble of making each individual relleno."

3 cans (7 oz.) whole green chilies or fresh Poblano chilies,
roasted and peeled. Remove seeds, stem, and open flat.

4-6 corn tortillas, cut into wide strips
2 cups shredded jack cheese (can use jalapeño-jack)
2 cups shredded cheddar cheese
8 eggs
1/2 cup milk
1/2 teaspoon each salt, pepper, ground cumin, garlic powder
1 small yellow onion, diced
simple salsa from a jar
1-2 sprigs fresh cilantro (Chinese parsley)
paprika

Begin by covering the bottom of a well-greased 9-inch square baking dish with chilies. Top with a layer of onion, cheeses, sprinkle lightly with salsa, and finally a layer of tortilla strips. Repeat layers beginning with chilies, etc. Build to three layers.

Beat together eggs, milk, salt, pepper, cumin, and garlic powder. Stir in minced cilantro and paprika for color. Pour mixture evenly over casserole. Bake uncovered at 350° until puffy and set in the center when lightly touched (about 40 minutes). Let stand for about 10 minutes before serving. Serves 6 for dinner, 10 for buffet.

POACHED SALMON WITH ZUCCHINI
Governor of West Virginia
Gaston Caperton

4 salmon steaks (1/2 inch thick)
2 tablespoons water
1/2 teaspoon chicken stock or flavoring
3 medium zucchini (1 pound)
1/4 teaspoon salt (optional)
3/4 teaspoon minced fresh basil
1/2 cup white dry wine or skim milk

Place salmon in large saucepan or skillet that has been coated with cooking spray. Add milk or wine, water and bouillon. Cover and bring to a boil; reduce heat and simmer until fish is done, about 6 minutes.

Cut zucchini into small strips; steam with a vegetable steamer for two to three minutes. Pour into a bowl and toss gently with basil. Transfer to serving plates. Top with salmon. Garnish with sprigs of basil.

DISAPPEARING MARSHMALLOW BROWNIES

1/2 cup (half 6 oz. package) butterscotch pieces
1/4 cup butter
3/4 cup flour
1/3 cup brown sugar
1 teaspoon baking powder

1/4 teaspoon salt
1/2 teaspoon vanilla
1 egg
1 cup miniature marshmallows
1 cup chocolate chips
1/4 cup chopped nuts

Set oven at 350º. Melt, then cool to lukewarm the butter and butterscotch pieces. Mix and add to butterscotch mixture flour, brown sugar, baking powder, salt, vanilla, and egg. Mix and fold into above mixture marshmallows, chocolate chips, and chopped nuts. Use a 9" square baking pan. Bake 20-25 minutes. Makes 12-18 bars.

WILD RICE CASSEROLE
Arne Carlson
Governor of Minnesota

"Luxurious wild rice was the staple food of the Indians of the northern Lake country of Minnesota and Canada. One of the world's rare flavors, it costs little to serve. An ounce of dry rice cooks up to a generous serving that lends an aristocratic touch to any meal."

Before the rice is cooked, it should be washed in cold water four or five times and any chaff or other seeds should be discarded.

1/4 pound butter
1 cup wild rice, washed
1/2 cup slivered almonds
1/2 pound canned mushrooms
2 tablespoons chives or green onions
3 cups chicken broth

*P*ut all ingredients except the broth in a heavy frypan. Cook, stirring constantly, until rice turns yellow. Place in a casserole and add broth. Cover tightly and bake at 325° for 1 hour. Serves 6.

Dijon Salad Dressing

1 tablespoon Dijon mustard
3 tablespoons red wine vinegar
1 tablespoon white wine vinegar
1/4 teaspoon salt
1-2 cloves garlic

1/2 teaspoon basil
1/8 teaspoon black pepper
2 drops hot sauce
1 tablespoon grated onion
12 tablespoons oil

Combine mustard and vinegars in blender. Add remaining ingredients, except oil; whirl until blended. With blender running, add oil, one tablespoon at a time. Chill. Keeps several weeks. Use on salad greens. (Yield 1 1/4 cups)

Mini Ham Loaves

2 pounds ground ham
1/2 - 3/4 cup Milnot
1 pound ground lean pork
garlic powder, pepper, parsley, to taste
2 eggs
(no salt is necessary)
1 1/2 cups fresh bread crumbs

Combine all ingredients in large bowl mixing well. Form into small oval-shaped loaves. Pour on sauce made by combining 6 ounces undiluted frozen orange juice; 1/2 cup brown sugar; 2 tablespoons vinegar after the loaves have cooked 30 minutes and juices poured off. Bake another 10 minutes with sauce over loaf. Makes approximately 30 loaves. Freezes well.

Party Rolls

2 packages yeast
1/3 cup melted oleo
2 tablespoons sugar
1 cup + 2 tablespoons warm water

1 teaspoon salt
3 eggs, beaten
5 cups flour
1/2 cup sugar

Mix yeast, sugar, and water until dissolved. Combine with remaining ingredients, except flour. Gradually add flour. Knead lightly; place in covered bowl and let rise for two hours. Punch down and let rise again until double. Roll out and cut to desired size. Let rise in buttered pans one-half hour. Bake at 375° for 10 to 15 minutes. Makes approximately 50 party size rolls. Freezes well.

SWEET POTATOES
Tom Carper
Governor, Delaware

2 pounds sweet potatoes
1 16-ounces can whole berry cranberry sauce
1/2 teaspoon cinnamon
2/3 cup self-rising flour
2/3 cup firmly packed brown sugar
2/3 cup quick cooking oats, uncooked
1/4 cup plus 2 tablespoons margarine or butter
1 cup miniature marshmallows

Cook potatoes in boiling water to cover 20 minutes or until tender. Let cool to touch. Peel and mash potatoes. Stir in whole cranberry sauce and cinnamon. Spoon into a lightly greased 2-quart casserole.

Combine flour, sugar, and oats, cut in margarine or butter until mixture resembles coarse crumbs. Spoon over sweet potatoes.

Bake at 375º for 20 minutes. Top with marshmallows and bake until golden brown. Serves 8.

"PLAINS SPECIAL"
CHEESE RING
Jimmy and Rosalynn Carter

1 pound grated sharp cheddar cheese
1 cup mayonnaise
1 cup chopped nuts
1 small onion, grated
black pepper to taste
dash of cayenne

MIX and mold with hands into desired shape (we mold into a ring); refrigerate until chilled. To serve, fill center with strawberry preserves. Can be served as a compliment to a main meal or as an hors d'oeuvre with crackers.

WITH BEST WISHES,

Jimmy Carter

AUNT EVELYN'S JOHNNY CAKES
OR MUFFINS
John H. Chafee
U.S. Senator, Rhode Island

1 1/2 cups corn meal
1 egg
1/2 cup flour
1 1/4 cups sour milk
1/4 cup sugar
3 tablespoons melted butter
1 teaspoon baking soda
1 1/2 teaspoons baking powder

Mix and shift dry ingredients into mixing bowl. Combine beaten egg, sour milk, and melted butter. Add to dry mixture. Stir lightly and pour into greased 9 x 9 pan or muffin tins. Bake 25 minutes in 425° oven.

CLAM CHOWDER

1 quart shucked clams or quahogs
1/3 cup salt pork, diced
1 onion, diced
4 cups potatoes, finely diced
3 cups water
2 cups milk
1 cup light cream
1 small can evaporated milk

Remove hard neck of clams and discard. Chop clams coarsely. Fry salt pork and remove pieces of pork. Add onion and cook until clear. Add water and potatoes. Cook 3-4 minutes. Add clams and cook until potatoes are done. Add milk and cream. Season to taste with salt and pepper. Better as it stands and seasons.

FLORIDA FISH
Governor and Mrs. Lawton Chiles
Florida

"The following recipe is a favorite of Governor and Mrs. Chiles. They are delighted to share this recipe and hope you enjoy preparing it."

2 fillets of sea trout or grouper
1 tomato - sliced thin
1 onion - sliced thin
6 medium fresh mushrooms - sliced
1 tablespoon of fresh lemon juice
1 teaspoon mayonnaise
salt and pepper to taste

Lawton Chiles

Cut a piece of foil large enough to enclose the fillets. Spray the foil with *Pam* (aerosol cooking spray). Place the fillets on the foil. Coat the fillets with one teaspoon of mayonnaise. Add lemon juice, salt, and pepper. Layer onions, tomatoes, and mushrooms on the fish and bring corners of the foil together to make a packet. Place on cookie sheet. Bake 20 minutes at 400º. Open packet and place under broiler until slightly brown. Fish is done when you can flake it with a fork.

GOVERNOR CHILES'
FAVORITE COOKIE RECIPE

1 1/4 cups (2 1/2 sticks) margarine
3/4 cup firmly packed brown sugar
1/2 cup granulated sugar
"Egg Beaters" = 1 egg
1 teaspoon vanilla
3 cups oats
1 1/2 cups all-purpose flour
1 teaspoon salt
1 teaspoon cinnamon
1/4 teaspoon nutmeg

Heat oven to 375º. Beat margarine and sugars until fluffy. Beat in egg and vanilla. Add combined flour, baking soda, salt, and spices; mix well. Stir in oats. Drop by rounded tablespoonful onto ungreased cookie sheet. Bake 8 to 9 minutes for a chewy cookie, 10 to 11 minutes for a crisp cookie.

LAZY CHICKEN RECIPE
Liz Claiborne
Designer

1 chicken about 2 1/2 to 3 lbs. (cut in pieces - 8 pieces)
3/4 pound small white or large yellow onion
1/2 pounds new potatoes or large potatoes
1/2 pounds carrots

2 cloves garlic - crushed
1 teaspoon powdered thyme
3/4 teaspoon salt
1 tablespoon butter

1 cup chicken stock
1/2 cup dry white wine
freshly ground black pepper
chopped parsley for garnish

1   Place cut up chicken skin side down in baking dish about 9 x 13.

2   Peel onions, if they are small, add them whole to the chicken. Add small new potatoes whole with skins, or peel and cut large potatoes in vertical quarters or chunks. Peel carrots, and again add ones whole or cut large ones into big 2-inch to 3-inch chunks. Tumble vegetables and chicken together so that pieces stick up a bit. Make sure chicken pieces are skin side down.

3   Sprinkle garlic, salt a generous amount of black pepper and powdered thyme over chicken and vegetables.

4   Pour in white wine and one cup of chicken stock. Chicken and vegetables should be half-covered by the combined liquids.

5   Dot chicken and vegetables with butter. Bake in upper third of pre-heated oven for between 50 minutes and 1 hour. Chicken and vegetables should brown as they become tender. Baste several times with pan juices, adding more chicken stock only if juices evaporate. Turn sections of chicken once so pieces brown on skin side.   Allow 10 minutes extra time for browning under broiler if necessary.

6   Remove from oven and check pan juices. They should be reduced by about half. If not, carefully spoon off juices and reduce in a sauce pan. Pour back over chicken in the baking pan. Sprinkle generously with parsley and serve.

•   *A cool green salad and some crusty, heated French or Italian bread, round this out nicely. (Yield 2 to 3 servings)*
•   *Use enameled cast iron pan - serve directly from the pan.*
•   *Cooking Time: 1 hour - preheat oven to 500º.*

CHOCOLATE CHIP COOKIES
Hillary Rodham Clinton, First Lady
The White House

1 1/2 cups unsifted all-purpose flour
1/2 cup granulated sugar
1 teaspoon salt
1 teaspoon vanilla
1 teaspoon baking soda
2 eggs
1 cup solid vegetable shortening
2 cups old-fashioned rolled oats
1 cup firmly packed light brown sugar
1 (12 ounce) package semi-sweet chocolate chips

Preheat oven to 350º. Grease baking sheets.

Combine flour, salt, and baking soda. Beat together shortening, sugars, and vanilla in a large bowl until creamy. Add eggs, beating until light and fluffy. Gradually beat in flour mixture and rolled oats. Stir in chocolate chips.

Drop batter by well-rounded teaspoonsful onto greased baking sheets.

Bake 8 to 10 minutes or until golden. Cool cookies on sheets in wire rack for 2 minutes. Remove cookies to wire rack to cool completely.

Hillary Rodham Clinton

WASSAIL
Dan Coats
U.S. Senator, Indiana

"This cold weather beverage is one of our winter favorites."

4 cups pineapple juice
4 cups cider
1 cup orange juice
1 1/2 cups apricot nectar
6 inch cinnamon stick
1 teaspoon whole cloves

Combine all ingredients. Bring to a boil and simmer 20 minutes. Strain before serving. Makes 10 cups.

SOUR-CREAM SUGAR COOKIES

"These are our son, Andrew's, favorite cookies. This recipe belongs to Dan's mother, Vera Coats."

1 cup butter
1 cup sugar
1 egg
1 cup sour cream
1 teaspoon vanilla

2 cups flour
1 teaspoon soda
1/2 teaspoon salt
1/2 teaspoon nutmeg

Cream the butter and sugar together. Add the egg, sour cream, and vanilla. Sift all the dry ingredients together and add to the first mixture. Chill for at least 2 hours--or overnight. Place on a greased cookie sheet by large spoonfuls, place a few raisins in the middle, if you like, and sprinkle with sugar. Bake at 400° for 10 minutes.

Grandmother Merrick's
SOFT MOLASSES COOKIES
William S. Cohen
U.S. Senator, Maine

1/3 shortening
2 1/2 cups sifted all-purpose flour
1/2 cup boiling water
2 teaspoon baking powder
1 teaspoon salt
1/2 teaspoon soda
3/4 cup molasses
1 teaspoon ginger
1/2 cup granulated sugar
1 teaspoon cinnamon

Place shortening in bowl. Pour in boiling water and add salt. Stir molasses and sugar. Add unbeaten egg and beat well.

Sift flour; measure and sift it together with baking powder, soda, ginger, and cinnamon. Stir into mixture.

Drop by spoonful onto greased cookie sheet. Bake at 375° for 12 to 15 minutes.

CHICORY & KIDNEY BEAN SALAD
a.k.a. *"Greens N' Beans"*
TIM CONWAY

2 heads of chicory or escarole
1 medium onion (sliced)
1 can red kidney beans
3 tablespoon olive oil
2 tablespoon red wine vinegar
salt & pepper to taste

Wash the chicory/escarole, discarding the tougher outer leaves (*unless you're an antelope*). If you have a lettuce spinner, give the greens a few whirls. Now pour the kidney beans and liquid into a bowl and mash lovingly with a potato masher. Put the chicory into a bowl and pour the kidney beans and their liquid on top. Add the sliced onion, olive oil, vinegar, salt and pepper, and then toss. Serve this salad with pita, Italian or French bread.

"Try it. I think you'll like it. "

RACHEL'S CRISP
The Washington Redskins
Executive Vice President
John Kent Cooke

2 1/2 cups tart green apples, peeled and sliced
2 1/2 cups ripe pears, peeled and sliced
3/4 cup flour
1 cup sugar
1 tablespoon cinnamon
1/4 teaspoon salt
1/4 pound butter, cut in 1/4" cubes

Spread the apples and pears in a lightly buttered 1 1/2 quart baking dish. Pour 1/3 cup of water over apples and pears. Put flour, sugar, cinnamon, and salt in a separate bowl, add the butter cubes and blend the ingredients with your fingers until the mixture resembles coarse crumbs. Spread mixture over apples and pears.

Bake for 30 minutes in a preheated oven at 350°.

Serve with vanilla ice cream while hot.

MRS. COORS SAUERBRATEN
William K. Coors
President, Coors Brewing Company

"Beer is an excellent meat tenderizer for all kinds of red meat, especially game. Sauerbraten marinated in beer was originally prepared by Louisa Coors in the late 1800's and is still a family favorite."

1 12 ounce can Original Coors beer
1 1/2 cups red wine vinegar
2 medium onion, sliced
1 4-pound boneless beef rump roast
1 lemon, sliced
12 whole cloves
4 bay leaves, crushed
6 whole black peppercorns, crushed
1 cup broken gingersnaps

1/4 teaspoon ground ginger
2 tablespoons cooking oil
1/2 cup chopped onion
1/2 cup chopped carrot
1/4 cup chopped celery
1 tablespoon sugar
hot buttered noodles

Combine *Original* Coors beer, vinegar, onions, lemon, cloves, black peppercorns, bay leaves, sugar, ginger, and 1 tablespoon salt. Place meat in plastic bag; pour marinade into bag over meat and close bag. Place meat bag in shallow pan. Refrigerate 72 hours, turning occasionally. Remove meat; pat dry. Strain marinade; set aside. Brown meat in hot oil. Drain off fat. Add reserved marinade, chopped onion, carrot, and celery. Cover; simmer 2 hours or till meat is tender. Remove meat. Reserve 2 cups of the cooking liquid and vegetables. Stir in gingersnaps and 2/3 cup water. Cook and stir till thickened. Serve with meat and noodles.

COWBOY BEANS

1 pound dry pinto beans
1 pound smoked ham hocks
1/2 cup chopped onion
1 12-ounce can Original Coors beer
1 16-ounce can tomatoes, cut up
1 teaspoon dry mustard

1/4 teaspoon pepper
3 tablespoons molasses
1/4 teaspoon pepper

Rinse beans. Combine beans and 7 cups water. Bring to boiling. Simmer 2 minutes; remove from heat. Cover; let stand 1 hour. Drain. Combine beans, Original Coors, and 2 cups water. Add ham hocks and onion; cover and simmer 1 hour, stirring occasionally. Remove ham hocks. Remove meat from bones; chop. Discard bones. Return meat to beans along with tomatoes, molasses, dry mustard, and pepper. Cover and simmer 1 hour more or till beans are tender, stirring occasionally. Add additional water or Original Coors, if necessary. 8 servings.

(More...)

BEER CORNBREAD

1 cup yellow cornmeal
2 teaspoons baking powder
1/2 teaspoon baking soda
1/2 cup milk
1/2 cup Original Coors beer
1 cup all-purpose flour
3/4 teaspoon salt
2 beaten eggs
1/3 cup cooking oil

In bowl stir together cornmeal, flour, baking powder, salt, and soda. Combine eggs, milk, *Original Coors*, and shortening; add to dry ingredients. Mix well. Turn into greased 8x8x2 baking pan. Bake in 425° oven for 15 minutes or till done. Serve warm with molasses, maple syrup, honey or butter, if desired. 9 servings.

Katie Couric's
LEMON LOVES
Co-Host, *Today Show*

C*RUST*

1 cup butter
1/2 cup confectioners sugar
2 cups flour
pinch of salt

*B*lend dry ingredients, cut in butter until mixture is crumbly. Press into an oblong (9"x12") lightly greased baking pan. Bake 20 minutes at 350°.

Filling

4 eggs
2 cups sugar
6 tablespoons flour
6 tablespoons lemon juice
grated rind of lemon

*M*ix with beater, eggs, sugar, flour and lemon juice. Add grated rind. Spread on top of baked crust and bake 25 minutes at 350°.

When cool, sprinkle with confectioners sugar. Cut into bite size squares.

Lite and *Lean* BEEF BROIL
U.S. Senator Larry Craig
and his wife Suzanne
Idaho

Served July 8, 1983, at the wedding luncheon of Suzanne and Larry Craig in Midvale, Ohio.

1 1/2 pounds Beef Sirloin Steak, Top Round, Flank, or Brisket

Marinade

1/2 cup soy sauce
1/4 cup water
1 ounce (2 tablespoons) lemon juice
1 ounce (2 tablespoons) honey
1 teaspoon instant minced onion
1/4 teaspoon garlic powder

Combine marinade ingredients in a non-metal pan. Add beef and turn to coat. Marinate beef for 24 to 48 hours in refrigerator. Broil beef to desired doneness (do not overcook; best served medium rare).

To Serve

Slice beef across the grain into thin slices. Sprinkle with sesame seeds. Serves four to six.

STUFFED ESCAROLE
Mario M. Cuomo
Governor, State of New York

1 head escarole
1 1/2 cups breadcrumbs
2 handfuls of grated Parmesan cheese
1 handful chopped parsley
1 clove garlic, minced very fine
1/2 cup oil
1 cup Fontina or American cheese, chopped
String to wrap around escarole

1   **Wash** the whole head of escarole very well. Remove the bad leaves. Mix crumbs, grated cheese, Fontina cheese, parsley, and garlic together. Stuff this mixture between the leaves.

2   **Pour** the oil over the top of escarole. Salt and pepper to taste.

3   **Place** in a pot with one inch of water (depending on the size of escarole, you can lay on its side in pan and tie with the string). Cover to steam and poach about 30 minutes, checking the water level from time to time.

4   **Serve**, cut lengthwise after string has been removed.

INSTANT MEATBALL SOUP
Alfonse M. D'Amato and his wife Antoinette
United States Senator, New York

"Fighting inflation at the supermarket may be the toughest battle of all for 'the forgotten middle class.' Most of the federal regulations that stifle business and private enterprise are passed right along to us - the consumer - in the form of higher prices at the check-out counter. Over the years, I have discovered that many of my family's favorite dishes are not only easy to prepare, but also economical. More importantly, they are flavorful and nutritious."

2 large carrots, peeled and cubed
3 large celery stalks, diced
1 medium-sized onion, diced
4 cups water
4 chicken bouillon cubes
1/2 pound ground beef
1/2 cup grated cheese, romano or Parmesan

*B*oil water in large saucepan or soup kettle. Add carrots, celery, and onion. Cover and let cook until vegetables are tender. Add bouillon cubes and simmer. Season ground beef with salt and pepper and shape beef into tiny meatballs (1/2 inch size). Add meatballs to soup, cooking from 3 - 5 minutes. Serve with grated cheese. Boiled pasta or rice may be added before serving. Serves 2 - 3.

PEPPER PORK CHOPS

6 medium pork chops   *3 green bell peppers, sliced*
3 - 4 vinegar peppers   *2 medium potatoes*
4 tablespoons corn oil   *1/4 cup vinegar (from pepper jar)*

*P*eel and cube potatoes and boil until slightly tender. In heavy skillet, add corn oil and pork chops to brown. Remove pork chops after browning, and add sliced bell peppers. Cook peppers until slightly tender. Add pork chops, potatoes; cooking for about 5 minutes. Add sliced vinegar peppers and vinegar to skillet mixture. Cover and let cook over medium heat for 5 - 10 minutes. Salt and pepper to taste. Serves 4.

(More...)

BAKED RICE

1 cup long grain white rice
3 cups boiling water
4 chicken bouillon cubes
6 tablespoons butter
1 green bell pepper, chopped
1 clove garlic, finely chopped
1/4 cup grated cheese, romano or any hard cheese

Melt butter in heavy skillet and evenly brown rice. In casserole baking dish, dissolve bouillon cubes in boiling water. Stir until completely dissolved. Stir browned rice into casserole mixture. Add cheese, bell pepper, finely chopped garlic, and ground pepper to taste. Cover and place in 350° oven for 30 minutes. Sliced mushrooms may be added before baking. Serves 4.

FRENCH-CUT STRING BEANS

1 pound fresh string beans
1/4 cup corn oil
5 tablespoons tomato sauce
1/4 cup grated cheese, romano or Parmesan
1 clove garlic, finely chopped
1 teaspoon oregano
1/4 cup water

Wash string beans and drain. Cut beans french-style (cut lengthwise). Place sliced beans in heavy skillet, adding water, oil, tomato sauce, oregano, garlic, and grated cheese. Salt and pepper to taste. Cover skillet tightly. Cook over low-medium heat for about 20 minutes, or until beans are slightly firm but tender. Serves 4.

"Enjoy these 'recipes for the forgotten middle class.' By sharing this collection of our favorites with you, I hope they will help ease the pinch on your family's food budget."

Antoinette D'Amato

CUPBOARD FRENCH DRESSING
Janet Dailey
Author

"A delightful dressing from the cupboard of the Ozarks' own Janet Dailey, well-known author."

1 medium onion, grated
3/4 cup sugar
1 teaspoon salt
1/4 teaspoon pepper
1/4 teaspoon paprika
1 cup vegetable oil
3/4 cup catsup
1/2 cup vinegar

Combine all ingredients in a screw-top jar; shake well.

Refrigerate to store. Makes 3 1/2 cups.

ROAST SUCKLING PIG
Tyne Daly
Actress

Between 12 & 14 pounds

Separation for roasting:

Soak for two to three hours in eight quarts of cold water, 1/4 cup vinegar and four tablespoons of salt. Clean inside ears, mouth, nostrils and scrub the feet...take out all innards and pluck any and all remaining hairs with tweezers. Remove the eyeballs...(cleaning thoroughly is important).

I put the following flavoring in rather than stuffing:

1 teaspoon of sage
1 1/2 teaspoon of allspice
1 teaspoon of thyme
1/2 teaspoon of clove
8 peppercorns

Mix all of the above together with one tablespoon of salt and rub it inside of cavity of the pig.

Cook:

Two cups chopped celery and two cups chopped onions. Cook both with a generous dollop of butter. Put this mixture into cavity of pig. Skewer the opening together. Place in a shallow roasting pan with a rack. Put a two-inch ball of aluminum foil into the open mouth and extend the front legs with chin resting on them. Fold back legs under the rump. Cover the ears and tail with foil to prevent over-crispiness. Set oven at 450°. Roast for 30 minutes. Brush with olive oil after 15 minutes. After 30 minutes, turn oven down to 350°. Baste again with olive oil and then once again 15 minutes later.

(More...)

*A*fter one hour:

Cup of sliced carrots, cup of onions, two whole garlic cloves and put into pan. Baste everything with olive oil.

---

*B*asting Glaze:

1/4 cup soy sauce
1/4 cup honey
1/4 cup dry mustard

Add two tablespoons of Worcestershire sauce and baste every 15 minutes for approximately two hours.

It is done when meat thermometer reads 185°. Turn off oven, let sit in oven for at least 1/2 hour.

Remove the skewers, drain remaining vegetables and place on a service platter.

Skim grease from roasting juice and add two cups of beef bouillon and one cup of port wine to the remainder of the basting sauce. Let simmer for approximately ten minutes.

Strain and then serve in a gravy bowl/boat.

*T*o Decorate:

Apple in the mouth, flowers and/or cherries or olives in the eyes and a necklace of green beans for the neck.

Add additional vegetables if so desired.

CHOCOLATE CAKE - FROSTING
Charlie Daniels
Musician

1 cup butter or margarine
2 eggs
3 cups sifted flour
2 teaspoons soda
2 cups buttermilk

2 cups sugar
1 teaspoon vanilla
1/2 cup cocoa
1 teaspoon salt

Grease and flour 2-9 inch layer cake pans or one large sheet cake pan. Cream butter, gradually beat in sugar until fluffy. Add eggs one at a time. Beat well about 2 minutes. Add vanilla. Add sifted dry ingredients alternately with buttermilk using low speed of mixer. Pour into pans. Bake at 350° for 35-40 minutes. Remove from pans after a few minutes. Cool on rack. Frost with Chocolate Butter Frosting.

CHOCOLATE BUTTER FROSTING

1 box confectioners sugar
1/8 teaspoon salt
1 teaspoon vanilla
5-7 tablespoons milk

1/2 cup cocoa
1/4 pound butter
   or margarine
   (room temperature)

Mix all ingredients together and beat on low speed until smooth. Spread on cool cake. This icing tastes better after it sits on cake for about one hour.

CHARLIE'S DIET CHILI

1 pound lean ground beef
2 cups sliced celery
1/2 teaspoon garlic salt
4 cups or 2 pounds cans undrained
      tomatoes
1/2 - 1 teaspoon chili powder

1 medium chopped onion
1/2 cup chopped green pepper
1 3/4 cup or 15 oz can undrained
      kidney beans
1 1/2 - 2 1/2 teaspoons salt
1 bay leaf

Brown ground beef and onions in dutch oven. Thoroughly drain. Add remaining ingredients. Simmer covered 1-2 hours. Remove bay leaf. Serve hot. Freezes well. 8 servings.
(1 cup - 156 calories)

SOUTH DAKOTA TACO SALAD
Thomas Daschle
U. S. Senator, South Dakota

"Makes a main meal on a hot day, as this is really a beef dish and a salad all in one.
A real South Dakota tradition on the plains!"

1 pound ground beef
1 head lettuce - chopped or torn
sliced tomatoes
8 ounces shredded cheddar cheese

1 package taco seasoning mix
1 can red kidney beans - drained
1 green pepper - diced (optional)
bottle Russian dressing

8 taco shells (or use crushed taco flavored chips such as Doritos)

Brown meat according to taco seasoning mix directions. Cool beef after adding seasoning.

Cut up lettuce, tomatoes, etc. just as you would for a garden salad. Mix all with cooled beef, beans, and cheese. Carefully mix in Russian dressing. When ready to serve, crush approximately 8 taco shells (or use crushed taco flavored chips, such as Doritos) and carefully fold the pieces into the salad for a nice crunchy taste.

Tom Daschle

NAMELESS CAKE & ICING
Dennis DeConcini
U.S. Senator, Arizona

*A Favorite Recipe of
Senator Deconcini's Family!*

3/4 cup shortening
3 eggs
1/2 teaspoon baking soda
3/4 teaspoon nutmeg
3 tablespoons cocoa
1 teaspoon vanilla extract
1/2 cup pecans,
    cut up and toasted

1 1/2 cups sugar
1 3/4 cups flour
1/2 teaspoon salt
1 teaspoon cinnamon
3/4 cup buttermilk
1 teaspoon lemon extract

Have all ingredients at room temperature. Cream shortening and add sugar gradually; cream thoroughly. Mix in well-beaten eggs. Sift flour once before measuring, then sift with other dry ingredients. Then add to creamed mixture alternately with buttermilk. Add flavorings and nuts and pour into well-greased and floured layer pans. Bake 350° for 30 minutes. Cool and ice with Nameless Cake Icing.

NAMELESS CAKE ICING

6 tablespoons butter
3 cups confectioners sugar
1 teaspoon cinnamon

1 egg yolk
1 1/2 tablespoons cocoa
1 1/2 tablespoons strong hot coffee

Cream butter and blend in egg yolk. Sift sugar, cocoa, and cinnamon all together and add to creamed mixture alternately with hot coffee. Beat until smooth. If necessary, add a few more drops of hot coffee so icing spreads easily.

APPLE MUFFINS
Mike DeWine
Lt. Governor, Ohio

Mix Together in large bowl:

2/3 cup flour
1 tablespoon baking powder
2/3 cup dark brown sugar
1/2 teaspoon nutmeg

In medium bowl, combine with whisk:

1/4 cup egg beaters (or one egg)
1/3 cup safflower oil
2/3 cup apple juice

In medium bowl, toss together:

1 tart apple, unpeeled and diced (1 cup)
1 teaspoon cinnamon
1 cup raisins
1/2 cup chopped nuts

Pour egg mixture over dry ingredients and fold lightly, 3 or 4 times with rubber spatula. Add apple mixture and distribute evenly using a few strokes. Divide batter evenly into 12 well-greased muffin cups. Bake in preheated 400° oven for 23-25 minutes.

CARIBBEAN TURKEY SALAD
Robert A. Ecker, CEO
Oscar Mayer Foods Corporation
Jennifer Cuccia, Test Kitchen Research Scientist

"It's a quick, refreshing summer dish, perfect for a picnic, party, or dinner with the family."

Salad:
1 pound Louis Rich, Honey Roasted, Breast of Turkey
2 cups cooked Minute Premium or Instant Brown Rice
1 medium tomato, chopped
2 celery stalks, sliced
1/2 cup golden raisins
1/4 cup chopped, salted peanuts

Dressing:
1/3 cup oil
2 tablespoons lime juice
2 teaspoons curry powder
1/2 teaspoon onion salt or garlic salt
1/2 teaspoon dry mustard
1/4 teaspoon hot pepper sauce

Cut turkey into 1/2 inch cubes. Place in large bowl with all other salad ingredients, except peanuts. Mix dressing ingredients and stir into turkey mixture. Cover and refrigerate (this can be prepared a day ahead). Stir peanuts into salad just before serving. Makes 6 (1-cup) servings. Preparation time is 15 minutes.

Louis Rich Oven Roasted or Hickory Smoked Breast of Turkey can also be used in this recipe.

HEALTHY HEART RECIPES
Governor Jim Edgar and his wife Brenda
Illinois

LOW-FAT CHILI

1/2 lb ground lean buffalo or sirloin
6 ounce can low-salt tomato paste
1 cup chopped onions
2 teaspoons chili powder
1/2 cup chopped green peppers (optional)
1/2 teaspoon cumin
8 ounce can low-salt tomato sauce
Brown sugar to taste (optional)
14 1/2-ounces of very low sodium beef broth (canned or dry)
2 15-1/2-ounce cans dark red kidney beans (undrained)

Cook beef, onion, and green peppers over medium heat until beef is well done and onion and peppers are soft. Strain all and run under hot water until beef loses oily feel when touched. Add remaining ingredients and bring to a boil. Reduce heat and simmer. Adjust seasonings to taste.

*Approximate composition per 1 1/2 cup serving:
325 calories   4.5 grams fat   60 mg cholesterol   40 mg sodium

POTATO WEDGES

4 potatoes (3 1/2 ounces each) - a combination of
brown and sweet potatoes is delicious
2 egg whites, unbeaten   Salt-free seasoning to taste

Preheat oven to 425°. Cut potatoes into wedges, for french fries - cut into thin slices. Dip wedges into unbeaten egg whites and place on a non-stick pan sprayed with vegetable spray. Season with salt-free seasoning and bake 25 minutes for wedges, 20 minutes for french fries, or until golden brown. Makes four servings.

*The Governor prefers to eat them as french fries while the
First Lady prefers the wedge cut.*

*Approximate composition per serving:
108 calories   0 grams fat   0 mg cholesterol   30 mg sodium

OVEN FRIED CHICKEN

2 skinless chicken breasts
1 cup skim milk
2 egg whites
1 tablespoon fresh parsley
1 teaspoon tarragon
1 clove garlic (minced)

2 teaspoons Worcestershire
dash of ground pepper
1/3 cup plain non-fat yogurt
1/4 cup corn flakes (crushed)
2 tablespoons corn meal

Soak chicken breasts in skim milk. Mix egg whites, parsley, tarragon, garlic, Worcestershire, pepper and yogurt. Remove chicken from skim milk and brush with yogurt mixture. Roll chicken in crushed corn flakes and dust with corn meal. Place on baking dish sprayed with non-stick spray. Bake in 375º oven for 45-55 minutes.

*Approximate composition per serving:
168 calories   6 grams fat   68 mg cholesterol   137 mg sodium

PEPPERY CHICKEN PAN GRAVY

2 cups skim milk
2 tablespoons flour
1 tablespoon chicken base
1/2 teaspoon poultry seasoning
chicken

1 teaspoon ground pepper
1 teaspoon lemon juice
1 tablespoon browned corn flakes/corn
   meal breading from oven fried

Combine flour and skim milk together in a container with lid and shake 1 minute until no lumps appear. Pour into saucepan and bring to boil. Stir until thickened. Add chicken base, poultry seasoning, pepper and lemon juice until thickened. Add browned breading from oven fried chicken. Serve with Oven Fried Chicken.

*Approximate composition per serving:
20 calories   1 gram fat   0 mg cholesterol   125 mg sodium

Jim & Brenda Edgar

Velvety Chocolate Cheesecake
Joan Embery
Goodwill Ambassador
San Diego Zoo

"Chocolate! Chocolate! Chocolate! This is one of my favorite things. Here is a chocolate recipe for your cookbook."

Crust: Make the day before for best results.

4 tablespoons butter, melted   1 cup graham cracker crumbs

Grease an eight inch spring form pan. Combine butter and crumbs. Press into bottom and sides of pan. Set aside.

Filling:
12 ounce semi-sweet chocolate chips, melted
3 (8 ounces) packages cream cheese, at room temperature
3/4 cup sugar
2 eggs
1 teaspoon vanilla
16 ounces sour cream
2 teaspoon cocoa

In food processor or with mixer, combine cream cheese and sugar until smooth. Beat in eggs, combine well. Add the cocoa, vanilla, and sour cream until smooth. Pour mixture into crust.

Bake in pre-heated oven at 350° for about 45 minutes or until edges start to puff and crack slightly. The center will still look uncooked. Cool to room temperature then refrigerate. To remove from pan, run knife around sides of the pan - remove sides.

FILE' AND OKRA SEAFOOD GUMBO
Secretary Mike Espy
Department of Agriculture
Office of Public Affairs

Secretary Espy was born and raised in the south. Gumbo is a Southern dish and has always been one of the favorite dishes of Southern cooking.

2 large red or yellow or white onions chopped finely
2 bunches of green onions chopped finely
3 medium bell peppers chopped finely
4 cloves of garlic chopped finely
1/4 pound of okra, cut into small wheels

6 bay leaves
2 pounds of peeled shrimp
1/2 raw oysters
1 pound of lump white crab meat
5 tablespoons of flour
2 cups long-grain white rice
salt, black pepper, and Tabasco to taste

1 fresh tomato chopped
5 cooked and seasoned,
  peeled crabs
2 tablespoons of file'
1/2 cup vegetable oil
chopped fresh parsley

In a large soup or stew pot over medium heat: Sauté the peeled shrimp in a vegetable oil. (Season the shrimp well with salt and pepper before cooking.) When cooked, remove from pot. Be sure not to overcook. Sauté the already steamed or boiled peeled crabs and claws in the same oil. Remove from pot after about one minute of cooking.

Next make a roux. Brown the flour in the vegetable. Watch closely not to burn. Keep stirring. Add the chopped onions and bell pepper. (Keep some of the green onions for garnish when serving.) Sauté several minutes until the onions and bell peppers are very soft.

While making the roux, keep water boiling in a separate smaller pot. After roux is ready, add water slowly. About four cups at the start. Keep stirring. Add the bay leaves. Keep the gumbo boiling over medium heat. Add more boiling water, to fill about 3/4 of the pot. Keep the pot at a very soft boil. Keep stirring. Add the chopped tomato, garlic, shrimp, crab meat, crabs and claws, oysters, and okra. Add salt and black and red pepper and Tabasco. **Don't be shy**. Add the file'.

(More...)

The gumbo should be cooked at a very low simmer for about one hour. Keep fire or heat low and stir. The gumbo should be soupy. Add water as needed during cooking. Add additional salt and pepper if needed.

Cook the rice: Two cups of rice should be cooked in 4 cups of water, 2 teaspoons of salt. (Hint: add a little olive oil to keep the rice moist and stop it from sticking.)

Serve: Serve the steaming gumbo over the cooked rice. Garnish with chopped parsley and green onions. Good with French bread and a salad. Serves 10.

Bon appetite.

A HEALTHY RECIPE
Chris Evert
Tennis Pro

4 cups chicken
1 cup pineapple chunks
1 cup celery
1/2 cup scallions
1/4 cup dry-roasted unsalted peanuts
1/2 teaspoon salt
2 tablespoons chutney
2 tablespoons lemon juice
1/2 grated rind
1/2 teaspoon curry
2/3 cup mayo

Blend well.

If possible, use fresh pineapple and low-fat, low-cholesterol mayonnaise.

AUNT VLASTA'S BANANA CAKE
J. James Exon
U.S. Senator, Nebraska

1 1/2 cups sugar	1/3 cup butter	2 eggs
4 tablespoons sour milk	1 3/4 cups flour	1 teaspoon soda
1 cup mashed bananas	1 teaspoon vanilla	

Cream butter and sugar. Add well beaten eggs and sour milk. To this add flour and soda sifted together. Then add the cup of bananas and vanilla.

Bake in long shallow pan at 350º.

Leave the cake in the pan and cover top with this icing:

1/2 cup sour cream
1 1/2 cup brown sugar
1 teaspoon butter
1/2 cup English walnuts

Cook to the softball stage. Beat and add nut meats. Spread before it turns firm. No other icing blends with the cake so well as this one given.

Russian Mayonnaise POTATO SALAD
Suzanne Farrell
of The New York City Ballet

2 yolks of hard-cooked eggs
1 teaspoon salt
1/2 teaspoon pepper
1 teaspoon dry mustard
1 teaspoon sugar (optional)
1 1/2 cup sour cream (real or light)
3 tablespoons olive oil
1 teaspoon lemon juice
1 tablespoon vinegar
red new potatoes

1 Rub yolks through a sieve.

2 Mix till smooth with salt, pepper, mustard, and sugar.

3 Add a little sour cream.

4 Now begin stirring in oil drop by drop, as with mayonnaise.

5 Put vinegar and lemon juice in last.

6 Pour over boiled new potatoes.

"Personally,
I like a little more mustard in this recipe!"

SAN FRANCISCO CHEESE PIE
Senator Dianne Feinstein
United States Senator, California

Senator Feinstein informs us that due to her extraordinarily busy schedule, she rarely finds time to bake. But when she does, she looks forward to making the following dessert "and eating it, too!"

Crust:

1 cup crushed graham crackers
3/4 cube melted butter
4 tablespoons sugar

Combine all ingredients and line in a Pyrex pie pan.

Filling:

4 cubes cream cheese
1/2 teaspoon vanilla
2 beaten whole eggs
1/2 cup sugar

Beat eggs, add vanilla and sugar, then add cream cheese cubes one at a time. Pour in prepared crust. Bake in oven at 375° until lightly browned.

Topping:

3/4 pint sour cream
1/2 teaspoon vanilla
2 tablespoons sugar

Beat until smooth. Bake, on pie, for additional 5 minutes.

Enjoy!!!

KANSAS APPLE DUMPLINGS
Joan Finney
Governor, Kansas

The Governor thanks PAWS® on behalf of all Kansans, "for the dedication, commitment and kindness you extend to our disabled."

pastry for 9-inch two-crust pie
6 baking apples (each about 3-inches in diameter), pared and cored
3 tablespoons raisins
3 tablespoons chopped nuts
2 cups brown sugar (packed)
1 cup water

Heat oven to 425°. Prepare pastry as directed except roll 2/3 of dough into 14-inch square; cut into 4 squares. Roll remaining dough into rectangle, 14x7 inches; cut into 2 squares. Place apple on each square.

Mix raisins and nuts; fill center of each apple. Moisten corners of squares; bring 2 opposite corners of pastry up over apple and press together. Fold in sides of remaining corners (as if wrapping a package); bring corners up over apple and press together. Place dumplings in ungreased baking dish, 1 1/2 x 7 1/2 x 1 1/2 inches.

Heat brown sugar and water to boiling; carefully pour around dumplings. Spooning syrup over dumplings 2 or 3 times during baking; bake about 40 minutes or until crust is golden and apples are tender. Serve warm or cool; if desired, top with sweetened whipped cream.

Makes 6 servings.

LINGUINI WITH RED CLAM SAUCE
Jim Florio
Former Governor, New Jersey

"Lucinda and I enjoy a number of dishes, but we do have a couple of favorites."

1/4 cup olive oil
1/2 teaspoon crushed red pepper
5 cloves of garlic, chopped
1 12-ounce cans of whole tomatoes, squeezed
1 small can of seasoned tomato paste
4 small cans of chopped clams with water
Salt and black pepper to taste
1 teaspoon fresh parsley, chopped
1 teaspoon fresh basil, chopped
for that Jersey fresh flavor cook down 6 Jersey tomatoes and add to canned tomatoes

Put olive oil, red pepper, and garlic in medium size pot. Brown garlic and pepper. Cool. Add all tomatoes and paste, clams, and water. Add salt, pepper, parsley, and basil. Simmer approximately 1 1/2 to 2 hours on low heat. Serve over linguini. If possible, make sauce the day before using.

STUFFED ZUCCHINI

4 zucchinis sliced in half lengthwise, pulp scooped out...
and chopped
1/2 cup mushrooms, chopped
2 cloves garlic, crushed
1/2 cup black olives, chopped
1/4 cup pimentos, chopped
1 tablespoon grated cheese
1 teaspoon oregano
1 cup seasoned croutons
1/2 cup white wine

In skillet, sauté all vegetables until soft. Stir in oregano, croutons, and wine. Fill zucchini shells with vegetables and crouton mixture. Bake covered with foil for one hour at 350º.

CHEESE STRATA
Nina Foch
Acting Teacher - Actress

Luncheon for Six People

Prepare the night before:

6 large slices sourdough bread
(cut off crusts if you want to, I don't. Pioneer is best)
10 1/4 inch thick slices Jack cheese (only Sonoma jack)
6 eggs
2 1/2 cups milk
1 tablespoon Parmesan (Reggiano if possible)
1 teaspoon salt
1/4 tablespoons cayenne pepper
1/2 teaspoon Worcestershire sauce

Make 3 sandwiches with cheese inside. Cut each in half. Place in flat baking dish which has been buttered or *Pam'ed*. Combine eggs, milk, and seasoning. Beat until mixed, and pour over sandwiches. Cover and refrigerate overnight.

In morning, turn sandwiches with spatula.

Before cooking... sprinkle with Parmesan. Preheat oven 350° for 10 minutes. Bake for 25 minutes - 30 minutes (brown on top).

Serve with light green salad and broiled tomato.

HOT DRESSED VEGETABLES
Ken Follett
Author

"Here is a way to liven up the vegetables that go with a roast dinner or grills."

You can choose any combination of vegetables that can be cooked together. For example: take a small cauliflower, half a pound of carrots, four sticks of celery, and half a pound of baby sweet corn. Slice the carrots and celery and break up the cauliflower into florets. Boil the vegetables all together until just tender.

Make a dressing with two tablespoons of lemon juice, six tablespoons of olive oil, and a little salt and pepper whisked together in a bowl.

Drain the vegetables, put them in a warm dish, and pour the dressing over.

JUGASEEDA
(Portuguese Rice and Beans)
Wayne Fontes, Head Coach
The Detroit Lions, Inc.

A favorite of Wayne Fontes, recipe of his wife, Evelyn Fontes, who is of Portuguese descent.

2 tablespoons butter or margarine
1 medium to large onion, chopped
1 bay leaf
2 cups long grain rice
1 16-ounce jar pinto beans, drained

1 tablespoon oil
salt, pepper and paprika to taste
2 tablespoons dried parsley
4 cups water

Sauté chopped onion, parsley, salt, pepper, and paprika in oil and butter only until onions start to turn clear. Add water and bay leaf and bring to a rolling boil. Add the rice to boiling mixture and stir. Cover and reduce heat to simmer for 25 minutes. Add drained beans. Recover and simmer 5 more minutes to heat beans through.

Variations: Canned and drained black-eyed peas, green beans, mushrooms, peas. **Frozen items may be used** (but should be added at the same time as the rice): lima beans, green beans, peas (10 ounce packages). **Fresh vegetables may be used** (but should also be added at the same time as the rice): Summer squash and mushroom cut in large pieces, kale cut with stems removed.

Dog Biscuits
Laura L. Douglas, Executive Secretary, The Detroit Lions, Inc.

1 cup white flour
1 cup whole wheat flour
1/2 cup wheat germ
1/2 cup powdered milk

6 tablespoons bacon fat
1 egg
1 teaspoon brown sugar
1/2 cup cheese, grated

Mix flour, wheat germ, powdered milk, and cheese. Cut in bacon fat. Beat together egg and brown sugar and add. Add enough water approximately 1/4 cup to make a stiff dough. Roll out on floured board and cut into shapes. Bake at 300° for 30 minutes. Turn and bake an additional 30 minutes.

Laura says that her two Golden Retrievers love these biscuits!

KENTUCKY PIE
Senator Wendell H. and Mrs. Jean Ford
U. S. Senator, Kentucky

1 cup sugar
1/2 cup all purpose flour
1/2 cup (1 stick) melted butter
2 eggs slightly beaten
6-ounce package of chocolate chips
1 cup chopped pecans
1 teaspoon vanilla extract
1 nine-inch unbaked pie shell

Mix together sugar and flour. Add melted butter and blend well. Stir in eggs, chocolate chips, pecans, and vanilla. Pour mixture into pie shell.

Bake at 325° in preheated oven for one hour or until golden brown. Serves 6 - 8.

Very rich

Wendell Ford

MISSISSIPPI MUD CAKE
and CHOCOLATE FROSTING
Kirk Fordice
Governor, Mississippi

"Mississippians Can't Get Enough of this Mud!"

1 cup butter
2 cups sugar
1 1/2 cups chopped pecans
Salt
Miniature Marshmallows
follows)

1/2 cup cocoa
4 eggs, slightly beaten
1 1/2 cups flour
Vanilla
Chocolate frosting (recipe

Melt butter and cocoa together. Remove from heat. Stir in sugar and beaten eggs, mix well. Add flour, pinch of salt, nuts, and 1 teaspoon vanilla. Mix well.

Spoon batter into greased and floured 13x9x2 inch pan and bake at 350° for 35 to 45 minutes. Sprinkle marshmallows on top of hot cake. Cover with chocolate frosting.

CHOCOLATE FROSTING

1 box powdered sugar
1/2 cup milk
1/3 cup cocoa
1/2 stick butter

Combine sugar, milk, cocoa, and butter and mix until smooth. Spread on hot cake.

MUSHROOM AND BARLEY SOUP
Estelle Getty
Actress

1 pound lean beef cut into chunks and some soup bones
3 tablespoons safflower or vegetable oil
12 cups water
1 cup barley
1/2 cup dried green split peas
1/2 cup dried yellow split peas
1/2 cup baby lima beans

(or eliminate one or more of the above beans and substitute any you prefer--lentil, pinto, whatever you like)

2 large carrots
1 parsnip
2 stalks celery
1 small onion, whole
1 small sweet potato peeled and whole
2 4-ounce cans mushrooms

Sear meat in oil until all the red is out. Place beef and bones in a large pot. Add water. Bring to a boil. Add all dry ingredients. Cook until beans start to get soft. Add all the fresh vegetables. When all is cooked add mushrooms and heat through.

Remove from stove. Discard parsnip and onion. Remove potato from pot and mash or purée then return it to the pot. Serve.

This menu may be adjusted to taste. Add whatever seasonings you like--salt, pepper, whatever.

MY FAVORITE CAESAR
Cynthia Gibb
Actress

6 tablespoons olive oil
2 cloves garlic, thinly sliced longwise
1/2 teaspoon salt
2 tablespoons red wine vinegar
1 tablespoon fresh lemon juice
1/2-1 teaspoon Coleman's dry mustard
1 dash Worcestershire Sauce
dashes fresh ground pepper
2-4 tablespoons fresh grated Parmesan cheese

Dressing:

In large wooden salad bowl, place garlic, salt and one tablespoon of olive oil. Mash with fork into a paste. Add remaining olive oil. Continue to mix while adding other ingredients in order.

Croutons:

Cube desired amount of Sour Dough French bread (without crust or crumbs). Heat wok or frying pan. Add butter. Add cubes. Keep them moving--when toasted, add a little more oil to moisten, then turn off heat and add ample amounts of that great old tune "*parsley, basil, sage, rosemary, and thyme*". Set aside to cool.

The Lettuce:

"*Don't be lazy!*"   Wash and then thoroughly dry one medium-sized head of Romaine lettuce. (Dressing won't stick if it's wet.) Tear lettuce into bite-sized pieces.

The Finish:

Add lettuce to bowl and toss. Add croutons. Sprinkle with a little more pepper and serve on chilled plates rubbed with garlic.

Cynthia Gibb

PEAS PORRIDGE HOT
PEAS PORRIDGE COLD
Whoopi Goldberg
Actress

1/2 stick butter
1/2 cup cooking oil, preferably French nut oil
2 onions, chopped
2 cloves garlic, chopped
5 medium sized potatoes, peeled and sliced
2 to 3 quarts chicken stock, preferably fresh
7 carrots, peeled and quartered
2 stalks celery, cut in half
1/4 pound French string beans (harticort vert)
3 leeks, cleaned and cut in pieces
2 large zucchini or 3 small green squash, cut in chunks
1/4 head fresh cauliflower, broken apart
2 bay leaves
pinch of nutmeg
salt and pepper
heavy cream

Optional: fresh parsley, frozen peas

Melt the butter in a large pot. Stir in the oil. Brown the onion and garlic in this, until golden. Add and brown the sliced potatoes. Add the chicken stock, all the vegetables, bay leaves, nutmeg, salt and pepper to taste. Bring to boil, then simmer 2 hours or more until vegetables are good and soft.

Remove vegetables from pot with a ladle and put them through a food mill, or bit by bit in a food processor or blender at low speed. Return them to the pot. Adjust salt and pepper. Dish out into bowls, topping each one with a generous tablespoon of heavy cream.

May be served in the winter, ice cold in the summer. Serves at least 12. A small sprig of fresh parsley compliments the celedon green color beautifully.

"Over the years, you will adjust this recipe to your own taste. I like to add a 1/2 package of frozen peas to insure the pale green color. A loaf of crusty French bread and, voila! You've got a meal for royalty."

Paprika Chicken with Galuska
Arpad Goncz
President of Hungary

1 chicken, about 1.5 kg (2.5-3 pounds)   *1 large onion*
1 tablespoon lard or cooking oil   *200 ml (1/3 pint) sour cream*
1 tablespoon flour   *1 tablespoon paprika*
1 small tomato   *1 green pepper, salt*

Fry the finely chopped onions, remove from heat and sprinkle with paprika. Add the chicken cut into portions, the salt, the slices of skinned tomato, and green pepper. Cover with a lid and stew over moderate heat, adding a little water from time to time.

When the meat is tender, add the flour mixed with the sour cream. Bring to a boil and simmer until the gravy thickens to a creamy consistency. Serve accompanied by "galuska".

GALUSKA

200 gr (7 ounces) flour
2 medium-sized eggs
2 tablespoons cooking oil
Salt

Work together the flour, the eggs, little salt, and sufficient water to produce a firm dough. Boil 5 pints salted water. In a pot, nip off small pieces of the dough into the boiling water using a pastry-cutter or a knife and a wet wooden board. Each galuska should be about 1.5 cm (0.6 inches) long, and you should only cook a few at a time.

When the galuska have risen to the surface of the water, lift them out, rinse them with hot water, drain, and heat them well in the oil. They should always be freshly made!

SPICED ROAST CHICKEN
Tipper Gore, Wife of
Vice President Al Gore

1 (3 1/2 pound) chicken
1 tablespoon margarine
2/3 cup Marsala

Mushroom Stuffing:

2 tablespoons olive oil
1 teaspoon garam Marsala
1 cup coarsely grated parsnips
1 cup coarsely grated carrots
2 teaspoons chopped fresh thyme
 salt and pepper to taste

1 onion, finely chopped
4 ounces button, brown or
  chestnut mushrooms, chopped
1/4 cup minced walnuts
1 cup fresh bread crumbs
1 egg, beaten

To Garnish: thyme and watercress sprigs

To Serve: seasonal vegetables
     Preheat oven to 375° (109C)

Prepare Stuffing: In a large saucepan, heat olive oil; add onion and sauté 2 minutes or until softened. Stir in garam Marsala and cook 1 minute. Add mushrooms, parsnips, and carrots. Cook, stirring 5 minutes. Remove from heat; stir in remaining stuffing ingredients. Stuff and truss chicken. Place breast down, in a roasting pan; add 1/4 cup water. Roast 45 minutes; turn chicken breast up and dot with margarine. Roast about 45 minutes or until a meat thermometer inserted in thickest part of thigh (not touching bone) registers 185° (85C). Transfer to platter, keep warm.

Pour off and discard fat from roasting pan; add Marsala to remaining cooking juices, stirring to scrape up any browned bits. Boil over high heat 1 minute to reduce slightly; adjust seasoning. Remove skin and carve chicken. Garnish with thyme and watercress sprigs. Serve with stuffing, flavored meat juices and seasonal vegetables. Makes 4 servings.

"I am pleased to send a copy of the Gore family recipe for Spiced Roasted Chicken. This recipe is one of my favorites. I hope you enjoy it too. Bon Appetit!"

WARM CRAB DIP
U.S. Senator and Mrs. Slade Gorton
Washington

"Elegant, yet quick and simple to prepare."

1 8-ounce package cream cheese, softened at room temperature
1/4 cup milk
1 tablespoon mayonnaise
2 tablespoons chili sauce
3 drops Tabasco sauce
2 tablespoons minced onion
1/2 teaspoon salt
1 cup cooked crab meat (Dungeness preferred)
3 tablespoons sliced green olives
1 8 1/2-ounce can artichokes (not marinated), coarsely chopped

*P*reheat oven to 375°.

In a mixing bowl, combine all ingredients except crab, olives, and artichokes. Mix thoroughly. Then gently fold in the remaining ingredients. Spread into an 8-inch baking dish. Bake at 375° for 15 minutes. Serve Crab Dip while hot, along with crackers or corn chips. 8 servings.

Award Winning Chili
Phil Gramm
U.S. Senator, Texas

2 pounds meat, part ground and part cut into sugar cube size
1 small onion, minced; or
1 heaping tablespoon of dehydrated onion

Brown and drain, if necessary.

Add:

2 (8 ounce) cans tomato sauce
2 (8 ounce) cans of water
4 tablespoons chili powder
1-2 teaspoons salt
2 teaspoons paprika (optional)
1 tablespoon ground cumin (optional)
1/2 to 1 teaspoon red pepper (optional)
2 cloves garlic, minced
2-3 tablespoons flour

Cook 1-2 hours.

Add:

2-3 tablespoons flour

Cook 15 minutes and **Enjoy!.**

ENGLISH TRIFLE RECIPE
Merv Griffin
Entertainer - Entrepreneur

sponge cake, plus one packet Italian Ratafia Biscuits
(if unavailable, 1 dozen macaroon biscuits)

peaches (2 cans or 4-5 fresh)
raspberries / strawberries (about 1 basket)
sherry
custard
thick cream (or whipped) (about 1 pint)
walnuts and fruit for decoration

Prepare in one large deep glass bowl:

Place sponge cake in bottom of glass bowl. Cover with a layer of ratafia (or macaroon biscuits). Soak with Sherry (1½ wine glasses).

Cover cake with alternating layers of fruit of your choice.

Prepare 1 pint of custard. (Available in tins made by Bird's Eye.) When custard is cool, pour over cake and fruit.

Whip cream until stiff and fold on top of set custard. Decorate with chopped walnuts and strawberries. Refrigerate.

IOWA CHOPS (Stuffed)
Tom Harkin
U.S. Senator, Iowa

1/2 cup whole kernel corn
1/2 cup bread crumbs
pinch of salt & pepper
3/4 tablespoon parsley
pinch sage
1/2 tablespoon chopped onion
1/2 cup diced apple
1 tablespoon whole milk
2 Iowa pork chops (thick cuts)

In a bowl, combine the first eight ingredients until well mixed. Cut a slit in the side of chop and stuff with mixture.

the BASTING SAUCE

1/4 cup honey
1/4 cup mustard
1/4 teaspoon rosemary leaves
1/2 teaspoon salt
pinch of pepper

In a separate bowl, combine the basting ingredients and blend until smooth.

In frying pan, brown stuffed chops and then bake in a 350º oven for about one hour, basting the chops often with sauce.

CARROT GINGER SOUP
Alan Hassenfeld, Chairman
Hasbro, Inc.

4 tablespoons butter
1 cup chopped onion
2-3 tablespoons grated, peeled fresh ginger
10 medium carrots, sliced (no need to peel)
2 1/2 cups chicken stock
1 1/2 cups orange juice
1/2 cup chopped fresh mint
salt and pepper
optional: dash dried lemon grass
(available at Oriental markets)

Melt butter in soup pot. Cook onions in butter 4-5 minutes. Add carrots and fresh ginger, stir to coat with the butter. Add the chicken stock and bring to a boil. Lower heat, cover and simmer until carrots are tender (about 40 minutes).

Purée the soup in a food processor or blender. Adding the juice and the mint as you process. Add salt and pepper to taste. Pour the soup into a clean pan and heat over low-medium until ready to serve. Garnish with fresh mint leaves.

Mr. Hassenfeld prefers this soup served deeply chilled on a hot summer day. To do this, simply pour soup into a container and refrigerate at least 3 hours or as long as overnight. Ladle into chilled bowls and garnish with the mint leaves.

Serves 4.

Chef Laura Johnston

SPRING LAMB SHANK STEW
U.S. Senator Mark O. Hatfield
and his wife Antoinette
Oregon

1/2 cup olive oil
1 large onion, chopped
1 teaspoon rosemary
1 1/2 cups chicken broth
4 large potatoes, quartered
1 package frozen string beans
1 cup water
1 cup white wine

5 pounds lamb shanks
1 teaspoon oregano
3 cloves garlic
6 carrots, cut in 2" pieces
1 package frozen peas
1 cup chicken broth
1 lemon, juice and rind

Poke one piece of garlic in each shank. Sprinkle with olive oil, oregano, rosemary, salt, and pepper.

Bake at 400° for 30 minutes, then lower to 325° for 3 hours and cover. After 1 hour of cooking time, add broth, lemon juice, and rind, water, and wine to shank pan. After 2 hours, add potatoes and carrots. Ten minutes before serving, add the peas and string beans. Serve over rice.

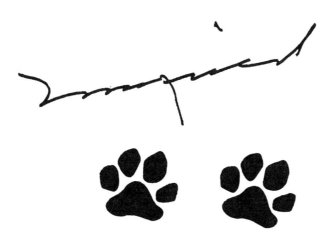

FRENCH ONION SOUP
Honorable RJL Hawke AC
Former Prime Minister of Australia

60g margarine
2 tablespoons wholemeal plain flour
pepper
wholemeal French bread

230g onions skinned and sliced
1 litre beef stock
bay leaves
low fat cheese sliced or grated

Melt margarine in a large saucepan. Fry onion 5-10 minutes till well browned. Stir in flour. Mix well. Cook 1-2 minutes. Pour in stock gradually. Add pepper and bay leaf. Bring to boil. Cover and simmer for 30-45 minutes.

Cut French loaf into diagonal slices 2cm thick. Toast lightly on both sides. Remove bay leaf from soup. Ladle into individual oven-proof soup bowls. Place slice of toasted bread in each soup bowl. Cover toast with thick layer of cheese. Stand bowl in tray and place under grill till cheese has melted. Garnish with chopped parsley.

POPCORN BALLS

Pop 1/2 cup corn in corn oil.
Boil 3 cups of rice syrup until it forms toffee.
Mix popcorn with 1 cup of natural sultanas.
Add toffee.
Allow to cool.
Form ingredients into balls.

Very sticky process!

FRUIT COBBLER
Jesse Helms
U.S. Senator, North Carolina

2/3 cup flour
2 teaspoons baking powder
1/2 teaspoon salt
2/3 cup sugar
2/3 cup milk
1/2 stick butter or margarine
2 cups sweetened fruit
(We use fresh peaches or blueberries)

Sift flour, baking powder, and salt together. Add sugar. Stir in milk just enough to remove lumps. Melt margarine in Pyrex dish. Pour batter into center of dish. Spoon fruit into center of batter. Do not stir.

Bake at 350º until cobbler has risen and is lightly browned.

Jesse Helms

SENSATIONAL SOUPS!
Heloise
Syndicated Columnist and Author

DOUBLE BERRY SOUP

"Some versions of this recipe add blueberries to the mix, and a West Coast variant includes kiwi fruit -- but they all taste great!"

1 cup orange juice, unsweetened
1 1/2 cups water
2 tablespoons cornstarch
2 cups fresh raspberries

2 cups cranberry-raspberry drink
1/2 orange rind, cut into quarters
3 tablespoons water
2 cups fresh strawberries, sliced

1/4 cup strawberry or raspberry schnapps (optional)
6 small mint sprigs

Mix the orange juice, cranberry-raspberry drink and water in a large saucepan (not aluminum), and add the orange rind (first remove as much of the white pith as possible). Bring the mixture to a boil and simmer for 2 or 3 minutes. Thoroughly mix the 2 tablespoons of cornstarch with 3 tablespoons of water in a cup and slowly stir this into the juice mixture. Keep the saucepan over the heat and stir constantly until the mixture is clear and thickened. Remove from the heat and take out and discard the orange rind. Add the sliced strawberries and raspberries, and the schnapps if you are including it, and stir thoroughly. Pour into a bowl, cover and chill for at least 2 to 3 hours before serving. Garnish with mint sprigs. Serves 6 at about 115 calories per serving, including the schnapps.

AVOCADO SOUP

A vegetable soup to serve cold. "For all you guacamole fans, here's another way to get your avocado ration!"

2 medium avocados
2 teaspoons lemon juice
1/2 teaspoon hot-pepper sauce
6 small sprigs mint

2 cups light sour cream
2 chicken bouillon cubes
2 cups water

Peel the avocados, remove the pits and slice. Put the slices in a blender container with the sour cream, lemon juice, hot-pepper sauce and water; crumble the bouillon cubes on top. Blend on medium speed until smooth and evenly colored. Pour into bowls and chill in the refrigerator for 2 hours. Garnish with mint sprigs before serving. Serves 6 - 200 calories per serving.

(More...)

TEXAS PINTO BEAN SOUP
Hot Stuff!
Hot Soup from Texas and the Southwest

It's only right that we include a recipe from Heloise's home state Texas! Here's a "hot" example"

"Like most zingy Texas or Southwestern recipes, you can adjust the amount of "hot stuff" you use."

1 tablespoon cooking oil
1/2 cup onions, finely chopped
1/2 cup green bell pepper, finely chopped
2 (15 1/2-ounce) cans pinto beans
1 (14 1/2-ounce) can whole tomatoes
1 (4-ounce) can green chilies, chopped
1/3 cup water
1 teaspoon cumin
1/2 teaspoon ground red pepper
salt to taste
1 jalapeño pepper, thinly sliced

Heat 1 tablespoon cooking oil in a large saucepan, add the onions and green bell pepper and sauté for about 5 minutes until the onion is translucent. Remove from heat and add 1 can pinto beans, including liquid, and mash thoroughly with a potato masher. Pour the tomatoes and liquid into a bowl and chop into pieces, then add to mashed pinto bean mixture. Add remaining can of whole pinto beans and liquid, chopped green chilies, water, cumin and red pepper, stir well and return to heat. Bring to a boil, reduce heat and simmer for 10 to 15 minutes, stirring occasionally. Serve with a slice or two of jalapeño pepper on top of each bowl as garnish. If this soup has too much bite for you, reduce the amount of ground red pepper and replace the jalapeño pepper with a teaspoon of sliced scallion. Serves 6 at about 155 calories per serving.

MISTY'S BIRTHDAY OAT CAKE
Marguerite Henry
Author

"Unfortunately, I don't have a recipe that would be appetizing for dogs or people. My favorite recipe in all the world is Misty's Birthday Oat Cake. Grandpa Beebe had established Misty's birthday as July 20th, so when the day came we always had a party.

"One time Misty ate the candles so we couldn't put any more candles on her cakes. Instead we cut off the tip end of carrots and stuck them upside down in the frosting. With their rootlets left on, they looked exactly like candles...lighted."

MISTY

Grease and flour:	2 nine-inch layer pans
Sift together:	2 ¼ cups flour
	1 ½ cup sugar
	3 teaspoons baking powder
	1 teaspoon salt
Mix in:	1 cup uncooked oats
Add:	½ cup shortening
Beat in:	2 egg yolks
	1 cup milk

After everything is well mixed, fold in 2 beaten egg whites. Bake at 350º for 35-40 minutes. Test with toothpick for doneness. When cake is cool, spread top with molasses and finely chopped walnuts.

Marguerite Henry

PIROK (RUSSIAN PIE)
Walter J. Hickel
Governor, Alaska

"This dish was brought to Alaska by early Russian colonists and was first made with salt salmon. Note that there is no oven temperature in the recipe. They used wood burning stoves and experience was the best teacher for temperatures. Ovens with thermostats are best set to 350 degrees."

Make pastry for double-crust pie. Line pie plate.

2 cups cooked rice
3 hard-boiled eggs

1 onion, finely chopped
salt and pepper to taste

1 pound fresh salmon, de-boned, or 1 pound canned salmon

When steaming the rice, add chopped onion. When the rice is done, mix with canned or fresh salmon (including canned salmon juice). Mix well. Season with salt and pepper to taste. Put half of rice and fish mixture into unbaked pie shell. Press quartered hard-boiled eggs into mixture. Top off with balance of rice and fish. Cover with pie crust, seal edges well, and cut steam vents. Bake half-hour for canned salmon (1 hour for fresh salmon) or until well-browned. Serve as a main dish.

PARMESAN HALIBUT

1 1/2 pounds halibut steaks or fillets,
cut into serving size portions
1/3 cup grated parmesan
3 tablespoons butter or margarine
2 tablespoons parsley, chopped
3 tablespoons of flour

Combine the cheese and flour. Dip the halibut in the mixture and sauté in butter until fish flakes when tested with a fork. Remove halibut from frying pan and place on platter. Pour the drippings over fish and sprinkle with parsley. Makes 4 servings.

FISH FILLETS IN SOUR CREAM SAUCE

1 pound fish fillets (halibut is good)
2 tablespoons minced onion
1/4 teaspoon dry mustard
2 tablespoons chopped green
        pepper (optional)
paprika

1 cup sour cream
1 tablespoon chopped parsley
2 tablespoons chopped dill pickle
1 tablespoon lemon juice
1/4 teaspoon sweet basil
salt and pepper to taste

Arrange fish in buttered baking dish. Salt and pepper to taste. Combine remaining ingredients and spread on fish. Sprinkle with paprika and bake 20-25 minutes at 375°.

CHARLESTON SHE-CRAB SOUP
Ernest F. Hollings
U.S. Senator, North Carolina

3 pounds lump crab meat (with roe, if possible)
3 tablespoons butter
2 tablespoons flour (for white sauce)
2 cups whole milk
1/2 cup cream
1/2 teaspoon mace
1/4 teaspoon celery salt
1 tablespoon Worcestershire sauce
salt and pepper, to taste
sherry, warm in a pitcher

Melt butter in top of double boiler and blend in flour until smooth. Add the milk, then the cream **very slowly**. To this add the mace, celery salt and Worcestershire sauce. Add the crab meat and fold **gently**. Test for additional salt and pepper. Add sherry to taste in each bowl. Serves 4 to 6.

Ernest F. Hollings

DELICIOUS "FIGHT BACK!" CHICKEN
David Horowitz
Consumer Activist

NO FAT--NO OIL--NO ADDED SUGAR--NO ADDED SALT

1 chicken (approx. 3 pounds) cut into serving pieces, skin removed
5 small white onions, peeled
1 cup canned tomatoes
2 tablespoons vermouth
Pepper to taste
1 large green pepper, sliced
1 clove garlic, minced
1 cup sliced mushrooms

Heat vermouth in large frypan. Brown chicken on all sides for about 15 minutes. Add all ingredients except mushrooms to pan. Cover and simmer slowly for 45-50 minutes.

Add mushrooms and simmer for 20 minutes, or until mushrooms and chicken are tender. Serves 4.

BOB'S BISCUITS
James B. Hunt, Jr., Governor
North Carolina

2 cups all purpose flour
2 teaspoons baking powder
1 tablespoon sugar
1 stick butter (cold and cut into 10 pieces)

1/2 teaspoon salt
1/2 teaspoon baking soda
3/4 cup buttermilk

Put all dry ingredients into food processor and mix for 30 seconds. Add cold, cut-up butter. Use pulse button and cut butter into flour mixture until the butter is the size of small peas. Transfer flour and butter mixture to a small mixing bowl and fold buttermilk into it with rubber spatula. Scrape bowl and put biscuit dough on floured surface, knead well (about 30 seconds). Roll out about 1/2 to 3/4 inch thick. Cut into desired shape (re-roll scrapes and cut them also). Brush with melted butter and bake at 375º - 400º for 10-15 minutes. Brush with melted butter when well browned. Split and serve with lightly sautéed North Carolina country ham or increase sugar to 2 tablespoons and sprinkle top of unbaked biscuits with sugar for the best strawberry shortcakes in the world.

MARINATE FOR FLANK STEAK
1 tablespoon tomato paste
1 tablespoon olive oil
1 teaspoon clove garlic
1/2 teaspoon course ground black pepper

3 tablespoons soy sauce
1/8 teaspoon oregano leaf

OATMEAL COOKIES
1 3/4 cup all purpose flour
1 teaspoon baking soda
1/2 teaspoon salt
1 cup butter
1 1/4 cup brown sugar
1/2 cup sugar

2 eggs
2 tablespoons milk
2 teaspoons vanilla extract
2 1/2 cups oats
1 1/4 cup chopped nuts
2 cups raisins

In small bowl, combine flour, baking soda and salt. In large mixer bowl, cream butter, brown sugar and granulated sugar (cream well). Beat in eggs, milk and vanilla. Add flour mixture, beat until blended, then add oats, raisins and nuts. Mix well. Bake at 350º for approximately 10 minutes.

A MENU FROM
HIS MAJESTY KING HUSSEIN
King of Jordan

"As His Majesty King Hussein's Lord Chamberlain as well as the President of the Jordanian Special Olympic Committee, I am delighted with the idea you are proposing concerning the use of pet dogs for the infirm and the disabled. Hopefully in the future we may be able also to benefit from your methods."

Prince Raad bin Zeid
Lord Chamberlain to His Majesty King Hussein

Menu

Appetizer
Cheese and fish canales

Salad
Mixed salad (lettuce tomatoes with cucumbers)

Entree
Kebab and meat balls, with rice and vegetables

Dessert
Peach Melba or ice cream

Beverages
Pepsi Cola, Perrier, Soda Water,
and tea

SWEET AND SOUR SPARERIBS
Daniel K. Inouye and his wife Maggie
U.S. Senator, Hawaii

3 pounds pork spare ribs
1/3 cup flour
1/3 cup Soy Sauce
3/4 cup vinegar
1 cup water

1/2 cup brown sugar, packed
1 teaspoon salt
1 clove garlic
1 inch ginger root
dash of Five spices

Cut spare ribs into 2" x 2" pieces. Marinate them in flour and soy sauce for 30 minutes. Brown in cooking oil. Add rest of ingredients and simmer for 45 minutes until tender. May serve with chunks of fresh or canned pineapple.

VIENNA WALTZ CHEESE CAKE

3 (8 ounce) package cream cheese, softened
1 cup plus 2 tablespoons sugar
4 eggs
1 tablespoon vanilla
1/4 teaspoon salt
1/4 cup melted butter
1 cup crushed swiebach crumbs

Blend softened cream cheese with 1 cup sugar, beating smooth. Beat in eggs, one at a time. Stir in vanilla and salt. Mix crumbs, 2 tablespoons sugar and butter; pat in bottom of 9-inch spring form pan. Pour in filling. Bake in moderate oven (350º) for 20 minutes. Cool. Spread with Pineapple Topping. Chill. Remove outer ring to serve. Makes 12 servings.

PINEAPPLE TOPPING

1 (8 3/4 ounce) can crushed pineapple
1/2 cup pineapple juice
1 egg

1/2 cup sugar
3 tablespoons cornstarch
1 tablespoon butter

Combine 1 (8 3/4 ounce) can crushed pineapple, 1/2 cup each sugar and pineapple juice and 3 tablespoons cornstarch. Cook over moderate heat, stirring until thick. Blend in 1 beaten egg and 1 tablespoon butter. Cook, stirring, a few minutes more. Cool.

(More...)

BANANA BREAD

2 cups sifted enriched flour
3/4 teaspoon salt
1 cup Hawaiian cane sugar
2 eggs
1 teaspoon lemon juice

2 teaspoons baking powder
12 teaspoon soda
1/2 cup shortening
1 cup mashed bananas
1 cup chopped macadamia nuts

Sift together flour, baking powder, salt, soda and sugar into bowl. Add to shortening, eggs and 1/2 cup bananas. Stir to combine ingredients, then beat 2 minutes at medium speed on electric mixer or 300 strokes by hand. Add remaining bananas and lemon juice. Beat 2 minutes more. Fold in 3/4 cup nuts. Pour into greased, line loaf pan 8 1/2 x 4 1/2 inches. Sprinkle 1/4 cup nuts over top of batter. Bake in moderate oven at 350º for 1 hour. Makes one loaf.

PAPAYA CHEESE CAKE

2 Hawaiian papayas, peeled, halved and seeded
1 tablespoon cornstarch
1/2 cup sugar
1 teaspoons grated lemon peel
1/2 cup melted apple jelly
Mint sprigs

1 lb cream cheese, softened
3 eggs
1 9-inch baked pastry crust
Kiwi slices

Purée one papaya half in blender to make 1/2 cup (turn motor on and off and scrape sides of container, as needed). Combine, purée with cornstarch; set aside in mixing bowl, beat cream cheese with sugar to blend well. Mix in eggs and peel; then stir in reserved papaya purée. Pour into crust.

Bake in 375º oven 25 to 30 minutes until just set. Cool. Top with remaining papayas, thinly sliced. Brush with melted jelly to glaze. Garnish with kiwi slices and mint sprigs. Makes 6 to 8 servings.

MAPLE SYRUP CAKE
James M. Jeffords
U.S. Senator, Vermont

"It is my pleasure to send you an old favorite Vermont recipe of mine."

1/2 cup shortening
1/2 cup white sugar
2 eggs (beaten lightly)
1 cup maple syrup
1/4 cup water
2 1/2 cups cake flour
1/4 teaspoon soda
2 teaspoons baking powder
1/2 teaspoon ginger

Cream the shortening, gradually add sugar. Add the eggs beaten without separating the white and yolks. Add maple syrup and water, then the flour which has been sifted, measured, and sifted again with the ginger, soda, and baking powder added.

Bake in a tube loaf pan about 50 minutes at 325°. Cover with maple icing and decorate with walnut halves.

James M Jeffords

GRILLED TUNA &
MARINATED CUCUMBER SALAD
Billy Joel
Musician

*"This is one of my favorite recipes
and should be started a day ahead of time."*

First Day

Marinate fresh tuna steaks overnight in the fridge in a mixture consisting of:

> *2/3 olive oil*
> *1/6 teryaki sauce*
> *1/6 lemon*
> *salt, pepper and parsley*

You should make enough marinade to completely cover the tuna steaks. The following day, grill the tuna steaks over a barbecue or open flame. **Don't over cook the tuna,** it should be pink on the inside.

Cucumber Salad

The cucumber salad should also be prepared a day ahead. Peel cucumbers and slice thin, combine the cucumbers with a mixture of:

> *white wine vinegar*
> *coriander*
> *salt*
> *pepper*
> *a dash of olive oil*

*"Some people like to add chopped white onions. However, if
your love interest is not sharing the salad with you, I
recommend that you leave out the onions."*

Second Day

After you have grilled the tuna steaks, break them into chunks and combine with the marinated chilled cucumber mixture. However, before you mix the tuna and the cucumber drain the cucumber salad and discard the liquid.

Bon Appetit!

HOT BROWN
Governor and Mrs. Brereton C. Jones
Kentucky

12 slices white bread toasted
12-18 slices cooked chicken
1/3 cup butter
1/3 cup flour
1 tablespoon butter
3 cups milk
1 teaspoon salt
2 egg yolks, beaten
1/2 cup freshly grated Parmesan cheese
12 slices bacon, cooked, drained

In each of 6 individual baking dishes, place 1 slice toast. Top with 2-3 slices chicken. Melt 1/3 cup butter and blend in flour. Add milk and salt and stir constantly until thick and smooth. Blend in yolks, then Parmesan and 1 tablespoon butter. Pour 1/2 cup sauce over each sandwich. Crisscross 2 slices bacon over each dish. Sprinkle Parmesan over all, run under broiler and serve golden brown.

CHILEAN SEA BASS
James Earl Jones
Actor

10 Maui onions
1 stick unsalted butter
12 pieces Chilean sea bass
   2" wide, 2 1/2" long
12 seeded, chopped roma tomatoes
   or the canned, drained or canned equivalent

5 chopped shallots
3 minced clove garlic
3 chopped basil leaves
1 tablespoon extra virgin oil
1/2 cup chicken broth (if needed)

Slice and cook onions in a skillet on low heat until caramelized (between 1 and 2 hours). Purée all ingredients except olive oil and chicken broth. Heat olive oil. Add ingredients and cook on low for 30 minutes. Add chicken broth as necessary. Season bass with onions and bake at 425° 10 to 12 minutes. Each of 6 servings should include one piece of bass over about 1/6 of the sauce.

Photo by Michael Jacobs

FETTUCCINE ALFREDO

3/4 pound uncooked fettuccine
boiling salted water
6 tablespoons butter
2/3 cup whipping cream
1/2 teaspoon salt
large pinch white pepper
large pinch ground nutmeg
1 cup grated fresh Parmesan cheese

Cook fettuccine in pot of boiling salted water for 6-8 minutes, drain. Return to dry pot. While fettuccine is cooking, place butter and cream in heavy skillet over medium low heat. Cook, stirring until well blended and bubbles for 2 minutes. Salt, pepper and nutmeg. Remove from heat. Gradually stir in Parmesan cheese until well blended. Return to heat if necessary for cheese to melt.

Pour sauce over fettuccine. Toss with fork until well coated. **Serve immediately.**

OATMEAL MUFFINS
Nancy Landon Kassebaum
U.S. Senator, Kansas

1 cup oatmeal
1 cup buttermilk
1 egg
1/2 cup brown sugar, firmly packed
1 cup flour (may use 1/2 cup whole wheat and 1/2 cup white flour)
1/2 teaspoon salt
1/2 teaspoon baking soda
1/2 cup oil
1 teaspoon baking powder

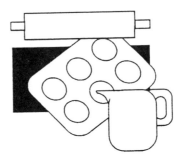

Soak oatmeal in buttermilk for one hour. Add egg and sugar, beating well. Then the sifted dry ingredients. Oil is added last. Divide into greased muffin tins and bake for 15 to 20 minutes at 400º. These muffins freeze well.

For a Healthier Version

The Center for Science in the Public Interest made the following modifications for a cookbook featuring recipes low in fat, sodium, sugar, and cholesterol:

Reduce oil to 2 tablespoons
Substitute 2 egg whites for the egg
Reduce brown sugar to 1/4 cup
Add 2 tablespoons honey for moistness.

"Whichever version you choose, enjoy!"

AVOCADO SOUP
The Honorable Paul Keating
Prime Minister of Australia

3 avocados
8g curry powder
salt
black pepper, ground
300ml double cream
900ml stock
15g lemon juice
cayenne pepper
chopped parsley

Chop the fruit of the avocados;

Blend the fruit with the curry powder, salt, pepper, and double cream;

Combine the stock and lemon juice, and add a little to the blender mixture;

Blend in the remaining stock mixture;

Pour the soup in a saucepan and reheat gently;

Season the soup to taste

Garnish each individual serving with finely sliced avocado, and chopped parsley.

CARROT-ZUCCHINI MUFFINS
BOB KEESHAN
CAPTAIN KANGAROO

3 tablespoons shortening
2 egg whites, lightly beaten
1 cup flour
1/4 teaspoon nutmeg
1/2 cup shredded zucchini (about 1 small)
1 3/4 cups quick or old-fashioned oats, uncooked

1/2 cup brown sugar
2/3 cup skim milk
1 tablespoon baking powder
1 cup shredded carrot

Heat oven to 400°. Line 12-portion muffin tin with foil or paper liners.

To make muffins, combine shortening and brown sugar in large bowl. Beat at medium speed with electric mixer or stir with fork until well blended. Stir in egg whites and milk gradually. Combine oats, flour, baking powder and nutmeg. Stir into liquid ingredients. Add carrots and zucchini. Stir until just blended. Fill muffin cups almost full.

TOPPING

1/4 cup quick or old-fashioned oats, uncooked
1 tablespoon chopped almonds
1 tablespoon melted shortening

For topping, combine oats, nuts, and shortening. Sprinkle over each muffin. Press into batter lightly. Bake at 400° for 20 to 25 minutes or until golden brown. Serve warm.

LINGUINI WITH MARANARA SAUCE
Sharon Pratt Kelly
Mayor, Washington, D.C.

Sauté 1/2 clove garlic and 1 onion in 1/2 cup olive oil
Add 2 cans of Italian tomatoes
Blend for 1 minute.

Then,

add 2 tablespoons fresh basil
2 tablespoons ground black pepper
2 tablespoons oregano
simmer for 1 1/2 hours

Add one can of minced clams and the juice of the clams.

Cook for another 45 minutes.

Serve over,

Linguini with Parmesan cheese
also serve hot garlic bread and butter.

MY BROTHER'S SALSA
Joanna Kerns
Actress

1 16 ounces can of cooked/peeled tomatoes
1 clove of garlic
1/4 teaspoon of salt
1/2 lime
1 ripe avocado
1 bunch cilantro
1-5 jalapeños (depending on hotness desired)
1 bunch green onions

In a blender, mix can of tomatoes (including juice), salt, lime juice, & crushed garlic clove.

In a pan with some oil, blacken the skins of the jalapeños. Take a plastic bag, put some water in it and then empty the water out--just to dampen the sides of the bag. Place the blackened jalapeños in the bag and place it in the freezer for about 5-10 minutes. Remove the bag from the freezer and pull off the skins from the jalapeños. Add the skinless jalapeños in the blender. Blend.

Chop cilantro and green onions. Dice the avocado. Place these three ingredients in a large bowl. Pour blended ingredients in bowl and stir. Enjoy!

LOUISE'S CHOCOLATE CAKE
J. Robert Kerrey
U.S. Senator, Nebraska

1 cup butter or Crisco
2 cups sugar
2 eggs
2 1/2 cup flour
1 teaspoon salt
2 teaspoons soda
1/2 cup cocoa
1 cup buttermilk
1 teaspoon vanilla
1 cup boiling water

Cream butter and sugar. Add eggs. Sift dry ingredients and add to creamed mixture. Mix well.

Add buttermilk, vanilla, and boiling water. Mix well.

Grease and flour a 9x13 inch pan. Bake at 375º for 35 minutes. Test with a toothpick for doneness.

Frost with a powdered sugar almond-flavored frosting.

CHICKEN ENCHILADA CASSEROLE
Bruce King
Governor, New Mexico

1 small can chopped green chili
1 large can Ashley enchilada sauce
1 can cream of chicken soup
1 small can Pet milk
2 cups chicken broth
1 1/2 dozen corn tortillas
2 cups grated longhorn cheese
2 tablespoons chopped onion
1 stewing chicken - boned and chopped

Sauté onions and chili in butter. Combine all liquids and add onion and chili. Break tortillas into pieces, place in casserole in layers with chicken and cheese, ending with cheese. Pour liquid over all and refrigerate overnight, or for several hours. Bake at 350° for 1 hour.

QUICHE LORRAINE

4 eggs	*1 cup Swiss cheese*
2 cups cream	*6 slices bacon, crispy*
3/4 teaspoon salt	*1/3 cup onion*
1/4 teaspoon sugar	*1/8 teaspoon cayenne pepper*

Combine eggs, cream, salt, sugar and cayenne pepper. Fry bacon until crispy. Layer bacon, grated cheese and onion in bottom of pie shell. Pour in remaining egg mixture. Bake at 425° for 1 hour or until table knife comes out clean.

Pie Crust

1 3/4 cups Wondra four	*3/4 cup Crisco*
1 teaspoon salt	*ice water*

BISCOCHITOS

2 cups Morrell lard	*1/2 teaspoon salt*
1 cup sugar	*1 teaspoon vanilla*
3 eggs	*1/4 cup orange juice*
3 teaspoons baking powder	
5 cups flour	

Cream lard, sugar, and eggs. Add vanilla and orange juice. Add baking powder and salt. Add flour. Can be put in refrigerator over night or made right away. Can be made with cookie cutter or with pastry gun. If made with gun, dip them in sugar and cinnamon after they are baked. If cut with cookie cutters, dip them before baking. Bake at 400° for 12 to 15 minutes.

BASIC BREAD
Stephen King
Author

"Baking bread is one of the ways I relax. I like kneading, and I love the smell of it, the way it fills the house and makes your mouth water."

2 packages of dry yeast dissolved in 3/4 cup of warm (not hot) water,
    with sugar as directed on the package
2 cups lukewarm milk
3 tablespoons sugar
1 tablespoon salt
3 tablespoons shortening
8 cups of flour, all purpose or bread flour
melted butter

Dissolve yeast. Add milk, sugar, salt, shortening, and half the flour; mix until smooth. Mix in rest of flour until dough is easy to handle. Knead on floured surface until smooth -- 10 minutes should do it. Put in greased bowl, cover with dish towel, and let it rise about an hour, until double. Divide dough in half, shape into loaves, place in greased loaf pans, brush with butter, and let rise another hour. Bake at 425° about 25-30 minutes, until brown. To test for doneness, tap to see if they sound hollow. Brush with butter if you like. (Yield: 2 loaves).

GAZPACHO
Ed Koch
Former Mayor, New York City

"The following is a recipe for the best gazpacho I've ever tasted, prepared and served at the home of Mary and Bruce Barron."

4 scallions
2 large cucumbers
4 large tomatoes, peeled and de-seeded
2 medium sized red peppers
1 teaspoon garlic salt
3 tablespoons olive oil
2 tablespoons red wine vinegar
Worcestershire sauce
Tabasco sauce
1 6-ounce can tomato juice
salt and pepper

*E*xcept for the tomato juice, put everything together in a Cuisinart -- adding the Worcestershire, Tabasco, salt, and pepper to taste -- until puréed. Place in any type dish. Then add the tomato juice. Place in freezer for 3 hours, stirring once an hour. Remove from freezer and serve.

Serves 10.

Recipe originally appeared in "Manhattan Spirit", September 2, 1993 and reprinted with their special permission.

BAKED BALTIC HERRINGS
Dr. Mauno Koivisto
President of the Republic of Finland

1 kilogram of filleted Baltic herrings
2 deciliters sour cream
3 deciliters cream
1 can anchovies
1 bunch dill
50 grams onion
30 grams butter
salt, white pepper, breadcrumbs

Peel and chop the onion, then fry gently in melted butter. Cover the bottom of a baking dish with the pieces of onion. Spread the Baltic herring fillets on a working top, season them and place half an anchovy fillet on each fillet. Roll the herrings up and place them in the baking dish. Mix the sour cream with the cream. Pour half of the mixture on the fish. Bake in the oven at 175° C.

When the herrings are cooked, pour the liquid from the baking dish, into a saucepan. Add the rest of the sour cream and the cream, thicken a little, season, and add the chopped dill.

Pour the mixture over the Baltic herring rolls in the baking dish. Sprinkle the top with breadcrumbs and brown quickly at 225° C. Serve with mashed potatoes made with butter or with boiled potatoes. Serves 6.

"A favorite dish of the President , since childhood,
as well as quite popular throughout Finland."

BEST-EVER LEMON PIE
and
NEVER-FAIL MERINGUE
Ann Landers
Syndicated Columnist

1 baked pie shell
6 tablespoons cornstarch
1/3 cup lemon juice
1 1/4 cups sugar
2 cups water
3 egg yolks
1 1/2 teaspoons lemon extract
2 teaspoons vinegar
3 tablespoons butter

Mix sugar, cornstarch together in top of double boiler. Add the two cups of water. Combine egg yolks with juice and beat. Add to rest of mixture. Cook until thick over boiling water for 25 minutes. This does away with starchy taste. Now add lemon extract, butter and vinegar and stir thoroughly. Pour into deep 9-inch pie shell and let cool. Cover with meringue and brown in oven.

NEVER-FAIL MERINGUE

1 tablespoon cornstarch   *2 tablespoons cold water*
1/2 cup boiling water   *3 egg whites*
6 tablespoons sugar   *1 teaspoon vanilla*
pinch of salt

Blend cornstarch and cold water in a saucepan. Add boiling water and cook, stirring until clear and thickened. Let stand until COMPLETELY cold. With electric beater at high speed, beat egg whites until foamy. Gradually add sugar and beat until STIFF, but not dry. Turn mixer to low speed, add salt and vanilla. Gradually beat in cold cornstarch mixture. Turn mixer again to high speed and beat well. Spread meringue over cooled pie filling. Bake at 350° for about 10 minutes.

CHICKEN PARMESAN
Frank R. Lautenberg
U. S. Senator - New Jersey

1 1/2 - 2 pounds boneless breast of chicken
one jar of your favorite tomato sauce
2 eggs
(can substitute egg whites if watching cholesterol)
1 teaspoon water
seasoned bread crumbs
8 ounces shredded mozzarella cheese

several tablespoons olive oil

Clean chicken breasts thoroughly, removing any fat. Pound breasts to 1/2 inch thickness with kitchen mallet. Set aside. Mix eggs and water in shallow dish. Dip chicken in egg mixture and then dredge through the bread crumbs. Be sure to fully coat the chicken.

Coat the bottom of a frying pan with olive oil and heat pan, being careful not to overheat. Place coated cutlets into pan and cook until thoroughly done (about 2 minutes on each side).

Once thoroughly cooked, top with shredded mozzarella cheese and cover with sauce. Place cover on the pan and heat until cheese is melted and sauce is hot.

"Serve with your favorite pasta
and garlic bread!"

RECIPES FROM
THE FAMOUS SENATE RESTAURANT
Carl Levin
United States Senator, Michigan

BEAN SOUP

2 pounds small Michigan navy beans
1 1/2 pounds smoked ham Hocks
4 quarts water
1 onion
butter
salt and pepper to taste

Take two pounds of small Michigan navy beans, wash, and run through hot water until the beans are white again. Put on the fire with four quarts of hot water. Then take one and one-half pounds of Smoked Ham Hocks, boil slowly approximately three hours in a covered pot. Braise one onion chopped in a little butter, and, when light brown, put in the Bean Soup. Season with salt and pepper, then serve. Do not add salt until ready to serve. Serves eight persons.

History of Senate Bean Soup

Whatever uncertainties may exist in the Senate of the United States, one thing is sure: Bean Soup is on the menu of the Senate Restaurant every day.

The origin of this culinary decree has been lost in antiquity, but there are several oft-repeated legends.

One story has it that Senator Fred Thomas Dubois of Idaho, who served in the Senate from 1901 to 1907, when Chairman of the Committee that supervised the Senate Restaurant, gaveled through a resolution requiring that bean soup be on the menu every day.

Another account attributes the bean soup mandate to Senator Knute Nelson of Minnesota, who expressed his fondness for it in 1903.

In any case, Senators and their guests are always assured of a hearty, nourishing dish; they know they can rely upon its delightful flavor and epicurean qualities.

[More...]

STUFFED CABBAGE

Combine:

> *1 pound ground beef*
> *1 egg*
> *1/4 cup uncooked rice*
> *1/4 teaspoon oil*
> *Grated onion or onion powder to taste*
> *Roll in steamed cabbage leaves*

Cook in 1/4 cup lemon juice and/or vinegar, 1/4 - 1/2 cup brown sugar, 1 cup tomato sauce, water or tomato juice to cover. *Simmer* at least one hour but as long as possible (as long as several hours). Can be frozen.

CARROT CAKE

This recipe is geared for a food processor; however, it can be adapted to a mixer.

1 cup flour	*3/4 cup sugar*
1 teaspoon baking powder	*3/4 teaspoon baking soda*
1/2 teaspoon cinnamon	*1/2 teaspoon salt*
5/8 cup oil	*2 eggs*
1 cup grated carrots	*1/2 cup roughly chopped walnuts*
Small can crushed pineapples (drained)	

Put all dry ingredients in processor and mix 5-10 seconds. Add eggs and oil and mix 30 seconds (will be very thick). Add carrots and pineapple and mix through. Add nuts and mix only to distribute. Bake in greased pan about one hour at 350º.

FROSTING

3 ounces butter

1/2 teaspoon vanilla

3 ounces cream cheese

6 ounces confectioners sugar (3 heaping tablespoons)

Process butter, cheese and vanilla for about 20 seconds. Add sugar and continue mixing. When cake is cold, pat all over.

Carl Levin

ARTICHOKE NIBBLES
Greg Louganis
Olympic Diver

2 6-ounce jars marinated artichoke hearts
1 small onion, minced
1 clove garlic, minced
4 eggs, beaten
1/4 cup fine dry bread crumbs
1/4 teaspoon salt
1/8 teaspoon pepper
1/8 teaspoon oregano
1/8 teaspoon Tabasco sauce
2 tablespoons minced parsley
1/2 pound shredded sharp Cheddar cheese

Drain marinade from one jar artichokes into medium skillet. Drain second jar, but save marinade for another purpose. Chop artichokes and set aside. Over medium heat, sauté onion and garlic in marinade until soft.

In a medium bowl, combine eggs, crumbs, salt, pepper, oregano and Tabasco. Mix well. Stir in cheese, parsley, artichokes, and onion mixture.

Turn into a greased 11x7 inch baking pan and bake at 325° for 30 minutes or until set. Cool slightly and cut into one-inch squares. Serve warm, at room temperature, or chilled.

Serves about 25.

AFTERNOON APPLE SNACKS
Mike Lowry
Governor, Washington

2 Red Delicious apples
1/2 cup chunky peanut butter
1/2 teaspoon ground cinnamon

lemon juice
1 tablespoons honey
6 whole graham crackers

Core the apples and cut each in half; cut each half into 3 wedges to make a total of 12 wedges. Dip wedges in lemon juice to keep apples from turning brown and place in a single layer in a microwave on high (100%) for 3 1/2 to 4 minutes or until apples are tender but hold their shape. (If microwave does not have a carousel, rotate dish halfway after 2 minutes of cooking.) Drain on paper towels.

In a small bowl, combine peanut butter, honey, and cinnamon. Snap graham crackers in half to make 12 square crackers. Place 2 apple wedges on 6 square crackers. Spread a layer of peanut butter mixture on apples; top with remaining graham cracker squares to make sandwich snacks.

TROPICAL APPLE SALAD PLATTER

1 Golden Delicious apple, cored and sliced
1 Red Delicious apple, cored and sliced
1 fresh pineapple, cored and cut into spears
1 honeydew melon, pared and cut into chunks
1 papaya, pared and sliced
1 banana, peeled and sliced
2 cartons (6-8 ounces each) low-fat lemon yogurt
2 tablespoons honey
2 tablespoons lime juice

Arrange fruits on a large platter. Make Lime Cream Dressing by combining yogurt, honey, and lime juice in a small bowl. Stir to mix. Serve fruit with dressing. Makes 8 servings.

Mike Lowry

LIME AND CILANTRO GRILLED TURKEY
BREAST IN PITA POCKETS
Richard G. Lugar
U.S. Senator, Indiana

"...one of my family favorites. To enhance the meal, I usually serve a rice dish and spinach salad. This is an excellent meal to serve at a summer outing."

1 1/2 pounds turkey breast tenderloins
2 limes, juiced

Rub turkey with juice of limes.

1 tablespoon paprika
1/2 teaspoon garlic salt
1/4 teaspoon white pepper
1/2 teaspoon thyme
1 1/2 cups lettuce, shredded
1 1/2 cups avocado salsa (recipe follows)
1 1/2 cups sour cream sauce (recipe follows - optional)

1/2 teaspoon onion salt
1/2 teaspoon cayenne pepper
1/2 teaspoon fennel seeds
10 pitas, cut in half

In small bowl, combine paprika, onion, salt, garlic salt, cayenne pepper, white pepper, fennel seeds, and thyme. Sprinkle mixture over fillets. Cover and refrigerate for at least one hour. Preheat charcoal grill for direct heat cooking. Grill turkey 15-20 minutes until meat thermometer reaches 170° and turkey is no longer pink in the center. Turn turkey tenderloins over halfway through grilling time. Allow turkey to stand 10 minutes. Slice into 1/4-inch strips. Fill each pita half with turkey, lettuce, avocado salsa, and, if desired, the sour cream sauce. Serves 10.

Avocado Salsa

1 avocado, diced
1 lime, juiced
2 tomatoes, seeded & diced
1/2 cup green onion, minced
1/2 cup green pepper, minced
1/2 cup fresh cilantro

In small bowl, combine avocado and lime juice. Stir in tomatoes, green pepper, green onion and cilantro. Cover and refrigerate until ready to use.

Sour Cream Sauce

1 cup sour cream
1 teaspoon salt
1/4 cup green onion, minced
1/4 cup green chilies, minced
1/4 teaspoon cayenne pepper
1/2 teaspoon black pepper

In small bowl, combine sour cream, salt, onion, chilies, cayenne pepper and black pepper. Cover and refrigerate until ready to use.

MOUSSELINES DE TRUITES "AMANDINE"
The Grand-Duke and the Grand-Duchess of Luxembourg

Mousse:

6 truites de 200 g.
2 oeufs entiers
3 blances d'oeuf
1/4 l de crême
1/2 l de crême fouettée

Sauce:

2,5 dl de vin blanc
100 g d'ammandes effilécs
1 dl de vermouth
2 échalottes
de l'extrait d'amande amer
le jus d'un demi citron

Garniture:

50 g de caviar
100 g d'amandes effilées grillées

1. **Préparer la mousseline:**
   - Lever les filets de truite puis leur enlever la peau.
   - Garder les arêtes et les têtes pour la sauce.
   - Mettre les filets dans un cutter (750 g environ).
   - Ajouter une pincée de gros sel et mixer en ajoutant les trois blancs d'oeuf puis les ouefs entiers.
   - Ensuite assaisonner d'un peu de poivre, de sel fin et de coriandre moulu.
   - Ajou ter 1/4 l de crême.
   - Réserver cette préparation au réfrigérateur.

2. **Préparer la sauce:**
   - Hacher les échalottes.
   - Faire cuire les arêtes avec le vin blanc et l'échalotte hachée pendant vingt minutes ajouter sel et poivre.
   - Faire bouillir la crême et les amandes jusqu'a épaississement.
   - Verser le bouillon terminé sur cette crême.
   - Passer au tamis et réserver.

3. **Cuisson des mousselines**
   - Fouetter un demi litre de crême et l'ajouter doucement à la première préparation.
   - Beurrer six petits moules à soufflé.
   - Verser les amandes effilées à l'intérieur; bein chemiser le moule et enlever le surplus d'amandes.
   - Ajouter la mousseline et cuire au bain-marie 25 minutes à 160°.
   - Sortir du four et laisser reposer pendant 5 minutes.
   - Démouler les mousselines retournées, ajouter 1 dl de vermouth à la sauce ainsi qui 1 goutee d'extrait d'amande et le jus d'un demi citron.
   - Napper les mousselines et garnir le dessus d'une cuillèrée de caviar.

4. Se sert très chaud, accompagné de concombres cuits ou d'épinards en branches frais.

CHICKEN MUSHROOM SOUP
Shirley MacLaine
Actress & Author

1 young chicken
1 clove garlic
1 teaspoon ground peppercorns
1 teaspoon soy sauce
Oil for frying

4 ounces mushrooms
1 teaspoon ground coriander
2 pints stock from chicken liquid
1 teaspoon monosodium glutamate

Cook chicken in water until tender, remove flesh and cut into small pieces. Re-boil chicken bones about 2 hours in same water. Strain stock.

Slice mushrooms, fry crushed garlic, coriander, and peppercorns in a little oil. Add mushrooms and chicken meat, including the liver.

Add stock and soy sauce; simmer 10-15 minutes. Add monosodium glutamate, stir well and serve. Serves 4.

Enjoy!

CHOCOLATE AND CHESTNUT GATEAU
John Major
Prime Minister of England

1O DOWNING STREET
LONDON SW1A 2AA

SPONGE CAKE

4 ounces **SR** (self-rising) flour
4 ounces granulated sugar
2 tablespoons milk
1 sherry glass of Van der Hum liqueur

4 ounces soft margarine
2 eggs
pinch of salt

Grease and line two 7-inch sandwich tins. Set oven to 350º or gas mark 4. Sieve flour and salt and beat together all ingredients for sponge cake until light and fluffy. Divide into sandwich tins and bake for 25-30 minutes. Allow to cool and spoon over liqueur.

CHESTNUT CREAM

1 pound tin chestnut purée
3 ounces unsalted butter
whipped cream for decoration

4 ounces plain dessert chocolate
3 ounces castor sugar

Cream together the butter and sugar until pale and fluffy. Add melted chocolate and chestnut purée. Beat until smooth. Sandwich sponge cake together with chestnut cream and spread on top and sides. Decorate with whipped cream.

CHICKEN BIRYANI
Nelson Mandela
President, South Africa

"Normally, Mr. Mandela is a very simple eater. He prefers chicken and fish, generally grilled and plenty of fresh vegetables, salads, and fruit. However, occasionally when he does stray from this, Chicken Biryani is what he chooses, cooked as follows:"

One large or two medium chickens washed and cut into portions. Add to this:

1 cup yogurt *4 whole green chilies*
1 teaspoon whole cumin seeds *4 cardaman seeds*
2 sticks cinnamon *1/2 grated tomato*
1 tablespoon lemon juice *some salt*
1/4 teaspoon saffron steeped in a little boiling water
1 1/2 teaspoons fresh garlic and ginger pounded together

In oil or ghee or mixture of both, fry till crisp and brown, 3 fairly large onions. Take out of oil and allow to cool. Crumble 2/3 of this onion into chicken mixture.

In two separate pots, partly cook in salted water:

4 cups of rice and
2 cups brown lentils, respectively

In a large pot put some oil or ghee at the bottom. Then add the black lentils, the chicken mixed with some of the rice and the juices, and the rest of the plain rice on top. Add the third of the fried onions that were reserved spread over the top and then pour over a half cup cold water. Steam. Do not lift lid till all liquid has been absorbed - about one hour.

This can be served with a variety of vegetables, salads, and pickles.

Mr. Mandela's favorite with this is as follows:

Yogurt and danya (coriander) leaves, mint leaves, garlic, and chilies mixed with ground cumin seeds and salt.

AUSTRIAN SPITZBUBEN
a.k.a. "Austrian *Wonderfulness*"
Penny Marshall
Actress - Director - Producer

1 cup butter
1 cup sugar
2 egg yolks
1 tablespoon vanilla
2 cups sifted flour
raspberry jam

Cream butter and sugar till light & fluffy. Add egg yolks and vanilla and beat well. Add flour; mix thoroughly till dough is stiff. Save 1/3 dough and chill for 30 minutes. Spread other dough in 9" x 13" ungreased pan. Roll other dough and cut in 1/8" strips. Spread jam and criss cross strips of dough on top. Bake in 350° oven for 25 minutes or till golden.

OLD FASHIONED BREAD PUDDING WITH CARAMEL SAUCE
Dal Maxvill
Vice President & General Manager
St. Louis Cardinals

*G*rease and flour baking dish.

*C*ut 4 cups of bread (white or whole wheat) into squares.

*B*eat 3 eggs and ½ cup sugar together.

*A*dd 2 cups milk and blend with eggs and sugar.

*P*our mixture over bread crumbs in baking dish.

*B*ake at 350° for approximately 1 hour.

CARAMEL SAUCE

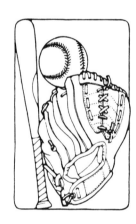

In saucepan over low to medium heat, cook:

1 cup brown sugar
1 tablespoon flour
Small amount of water

Then add:

A little vanilla
Dash of salt
Lump of butter or margarine

Pour warm sauce over cooled bread pudding and *serve!*

ARIZONA BAKED BEANS
John McCain
United States Senator, Arizona

1 16-ounce can red kidney beans
1 16 -ounce can B&M Baked Beans
1 cup ketchup
1 cup packed brown sugar
1 medium onion - chopped
1 tablespoon vinegar
1 teaspoon yellow French's mustard
4 strips fried bacon, cooled and crumbled

In a skillet, sauté chopped onion with a teaspoon or so of butter. In a large baking pot, combine kidney beans, B&M Baked Beans, ketchup, brown sugar, vinegar, mustard, and crumbled bacon. After combining and stirring enough to mix the ingredients, add the sautéed onion. Mix well.

Bake in a covered dish at 350º-375º for 35 minutes or until piping hot.

"This dish is perfect with barbecued foods...Enjoy!"

John McCain

Rue's True-Blue
RED HOT VEGETARIAN CHILI
Rue McClanahan
Actress

1 pound firm tofu, squashed
3 tablespoons cooking oil
2 large onions, minced
1 green or red pepper, minced
3 or 4 sections of garlic
4 or 5 tablespoons chili powder
8 ounces mushrooms
1/4 teaspoon cayenne
1/4 teaspoon cumin
salt and pepper to taste
52 ounces kidney beans
29 ounces tomato sauce
29 ounces whole peeled tomatoes (or fresh, peeled)

Heat oil in heavy pot. Cook tofu 3 minutes. Add onions, pepper, garlic, chili powder, cumin, mushrooms, and cayenne. *Cook* over medium heat 7-8 minutes. Add tomatoes, sauce, and beans. *Simmer* at least one hour. Salt & pepper to taste while cooking.

Serve with rice or crackers or both.

BURGOO
Mitch McConnell, U.S. Senator, Kentucky

"Burgoo is a stew-like dish from Kentucky served often at large gatherings of family and friends. Derby is a particularly popular occasion to serve this dish, which is a meal in itself. It takes two days to prepare, but do not let that scare you: the final product is worth the wait. This is best made when fresh vegetables are at their peak, but frozen vegetables and canned tomatoes can be used when necessary. It freezes well. If you make this in 2 parts, on successive days, it is not such a chore."

1 4-to-5 pound hen
1 pound beef stew meat
1 pound veal stew meat
4 large beef or knuckle bones
celery, carrot, onion, parsley
1 can (10 ounces) tomato purée
4 quarts water
1 red pepper pod
1/4 cup salt
1 tablespoon each lemon juice
   Worcestershire, sugar, salt
1 1/2 teaspoons course black
   pepper
1/2 teaspoon cayenne

6 onions, finely chopped
2 green peppers, finely chopped
1 medium turnip, finely diced
8-10 tomatoes, peeled
chopped
2 cups shelled fresh
butterbeans
2 cups thinly sliced celery
2 cups finely chopped cabbage

2 cups fresh okra, sliced

2 cups fresh corn (6 ears)
2 unpeeled lemon, seeded

Put all the ingredients in the first column in a roaster, bring to a boil and simmer slowly, covered, for about 4 hours. Let cool and strain. Cut chicken and meat fine, removing all skin, bone, and gristle. Scissors are good for this job. Return to stock and refrigerate. The following day, lift off half the fat, add all the vegetables except corn and okra, sautéing first the onions and green peppers in a little bacon fat or butter. Simmer slowly for an hour, covered. Uncover, add okra and cook another hour or until thick. Cut corn twice, scraping to get the milk. Add this along with the lemon and additional seasonings. If you finish the cooking in the oven, it will eliminate stirring and watching. Cook, uncovered, at 300° for about 2 hours until the consistency of a thick stew. This will make a gallon. If made beforehand, reheat in the oven to insure against scorching. Serve in mugs and sprinkle with chopped fresh parsley.

HOPPIN' JOHN

1/4 pound of slab bacon
2 cups uncooked regular rice
2 cups fresh or frozen black-eyed peas
salt to taste
2 small pods red peppers

Cover peas with water. Simmer peas, bacon and peppers in a covered pot over low heat for 1 to 1 1/2 hours, or until tender. Add rice, cover and cook over low heat, stirring frequently until rice is cooked. Add more water during cooking if necessary. Add salt to desired taste. Yield: 8 servings.

TROPICAL RAIN FOREST GRANOLA
Danica McKellar
Actress

"First of all, get all of your ingredients as fresh as possible and also organically grown. The use of pesticides and other poisons pollutes our waterways and oceans as well as the foods we eat, the air we breathe and other animal, fish and friendly insect life. I buy organically grown products whenever they're available, as well as growing my own! Next, by buying and adding products that come from the Rain Forests to this recipe and in other areas of our lives, we help to create jobs in the Rain Forests that promote the protection, not the destruction, of the trees and other native life. This Earth-conscious and healthy snack is one of my all-time favorites!"

Preheat oven to 225° F.

In a large container mix the following:

6 cups rolled oats (not instant)
1 cup chopped Brazil nuts*
1 cup cashew nuts*
1 cup raw sunflower seeds
1 cup chopped pecans
1 cup pumpkin seeds
1 cup flax seed
1 cup oat bran
1 cup Millers bran flakes
1 cup chopped almonds
1 cup sesame seeds

Photo by Ann Bogart

(all nuts and seeds are shelled and unsalted)

In a sauce pan warm the following:

> *2 1/2 cups honey*
> *1 3/4 cups safflower oil*
> *1 1/2 teaspoons real vanilla extract (not vanillin)*
> *1/4 cup molasses*

Mix warm ingredients into dry ingredients until everything is coated.

Spread evenly on baking pans & bake at 225° for 1/2 hour.

Stir ingredients on pans so they will brown evenly.

Bake for 1/2 hour longer or until nicely browned.

Serve your Tropical Rain Forest Granola as a snack or for breakfast with milk and a glass of cupuassu*, calamansi*, or guanabana* juice.
(Note: *   is a product of the Tropical Rain Forests.)

MAINE LOBSTER CASSEROLE
John R. McKernan, Jr.
Governor, State of Maine

1 1/2 pounds Maine lobster	*4 tablespoons butter*
4 tablespoons sherry	*4 tablespoons brandy*
3-4 tablespoons flour	*salt*
paprika	*3/4 teaspoons dry mustard*
1 pint all purpose cream	*5 pieces bread (crust removed)*

Cut Maine lobster into bite size pieces, sauté lightly. Make a sauce of butter, flour, dry mustard, salt, paprika, and 1/2 of the cream. Mix with seafood and add bread which has been cut into small cube. Add reserved cream to give medium thickness. Add sherry and brandy. Pour into flat baking dish.

> **Topping:** Process one stack of Ritz crackers until crushed fine. Mix with stick of melted butter and heat until lightly brown. Spread over casserole.

Bake at 325° for 20 minutes until top is brown and bubbling. Serves 8.

MAINE WILD BLUEBERRY COBBLER

1 pint Maine wild blueberries	*1/3 cup water*
1 cup white sugar	*1 teaspoon grated lemon rind*
1 cup flour	*1/4 cup brown sugar*
1 teaspoon baking powder	*1 1/2 tablespoons cinnamon*
1/3 cup butter	

Preheat oven to 350°. Combine Maine wild blueberries, 3/4 cut white sugar, water, and lemon rind in a baking dish. Bring to a boil and simmer for 2 minutes.

Meanwhile, combine reserved 1/4 cup white sugar with brown sugar, flour, baking powder, and cinnamon. Cut in butter until mixture is crumbly. Sprinkle crumbs over blueberry mixture. Bake approximately 25 minutes or until top is brown. Serve warm with heavy cream or vanilla ice cream.

TENNESSEE CHILI
Ned McWherter
Governor, State of Tennessee

"...I am pleased to enclose a recipe for Tennessee Chili, which was my late mother's favorite."

2 teaspoons butter or margarine
3 pounds beef chuck, cut into ½" pieces
1 large onion
1 green pepper, chopped
1 garlic clove, crushed
4-6 tablespoons chili powder
2 bay leaves
2 teaspoons each oregano and sugar
1 teaspoon each cumin and salt
½ teaspoon freshly ground pepper
1 can (14 ¼ or 16 ounces) stewed tomatoes
1 can (13 ¾ or 14 ½ ounces) beef broth
1 can (16 ounces) red kidney beans, drained and rinsed
1 can (16 ounces) tomato sauce
1 cup water
1 tablespoon cornmeal

In Dutch oven melt butter or margarine over high heat. Add beef and brown. Drain excess fat. Stir in onion, green pepper, and garlic; sauté until vegetables are softened, 3 minutes. Stir in next 7 ingredients; cook 2 minutes. Add remaining ingredients. Bring to a boil; reduce heat, cover and simmer 1 hour. Simmer uncovered 1 - 1½ hours more. Discard garlic and bay leaves.

Makes 2 quarts, 660 calories per cup.

This favorite recipe of Governor McWherter's mother, Lucille, won Honorable Mention in the 1988 Ladies' Home Journal 'Great Chili Cook-Off'.

EMPANADAS CRIOLLAS - RELLENO
Carlos Saul Menem, Presidencia de la Nación
Argentina

Empanadas Criollas
4 tazas de harina (1/2 kilo)
3 cucharaditas de polvo leudante
2 1/2 cucharaditas de sal
3/4 taza de manteca derretida, fría
1 yema
1 taza de agua fría (1/4 litro)

Relleno
1/2 taza de aceite
1 cebolla blanca, picada
4 cebollitas de verdeo, picadas
1 ají verde, dulce, picado
*3 tomates, pelados y sin
   semillas*
3 cucharadas de caldo
1 hoja de laurel
1/4 de cucharadita de orégano
1 1/2 cucharadita de sal
1/4 cucharadita de pimienta
1/2 cucharadita de ají molido
*1/2 kilo de carnaza de ternera,
   picada*
1/4 cucharadita comino molido
*3 huevos duros, cortados en
   cascos*
*15 aceitunas verdes,
   descarozadas*
*1/4 de taza de pasas sin
   semillas*

Realizacion:
Se tamizan juntos sobre la mesa, la harina, el polvo leudante y la sal. Se hace un hueco en el centro, en el que se ponen la manteca, la yema y el agua. Se mezclan estos tres elementos con un tenedor y luego se les va haciendo tomar los ingredientes secos. Se amasa bien hasta que quede una masa lisa y se estira, dejándola fina (2 mms). Se marcan redondeles con un plato de té, se cortan con un cuchillo y se les pone en el centro una cucharada colmada de relleno. Se pintan los bordes con agua, se cierran las empanadas y se les hace un repulgo. Se fríen en abundante aceite que deberá estar tibio cuando se echan las empanadas, aumentando el calor a medida que se van cocinando. También se pueden hornear, pintadas previamente con huevo batido.

RELLANO: En una cacerola se pone el aceite al fuego y cuando está caliente, se echan las cebollas y el ají; cuando comienzan a dorarse se echan los tomates, el caldo, el laurel, el orégano, la sal, la pimienta y el ají molido y se dejan cocinar a calor suave durante 30 minutos más. Aparte, en un recipiente, se pone la carne, cubriéndola con agua hirviendo, se revuelve y se cuela. Cuando la salsa está preparada, se retira del fuego y se le une la carne y el comino. Se extiende la preparación en una fuente baja y se deja enfriar. Por encima se le ponen los huevos duros, las aceitunas y las pasas, pasadas previamente por agua hirviendo, todo en forma pareja.

CHOCOLATE CAKE WITH FRESH RASPBERRIES
Stephen Merrill *and his wife* Heather
Governor, New Hampshire

1 cup boiling water
1 stick of butter
2 cups sugar
1 teaspoon vanilla
1/2 cup sour cream
1 teaspoon baking powder sifted

3 ounces unsweetened chocolate
1 teaspoon vanilla
2 eggs, separated
1 teaspoon baking soda
2 cups less 2 tablespoons flour

Preheat oven to 350°. Grease and flour 10-inch spring form pan. Pour boiling water over chocolate and butter. When melted, stir in vanilla and sugar, then whisk in egg yolks, one at a time. Mix baking soda and sour cream and whisk into chocolate mixture. Sift flour and baking soda together, add to batter. Beat egg whites until stiff. Stir a quarter of the egg whites into the batter. Fold remaining egg whites into the batter. Pour batter in pan. Place on middle rack in oven, bake 40-50 minutes or until a cake tester inserted into the middle comes out clean. Cool, remove from pan.

Frosting

2 tablespoons butter
1 teaspoon vanilla
1 ¼ cup sifted confectioners sugar

6 tablespoons heavy cream
¾ cup chocolate chips

Place all ingredients in a heavy sauce pan over low heat and whisk until smooth. Cool slightly, add more sugar if necessary. Spread on cake while frosting is still warm. Top with fresh raspberries.

Mount Diablo Dip

3 or 4 ripe avocados
1 16 ounces container sour cream
2 ripe tomatoes, chopped
8 oz Monterey Jack cheese, grated
1 large bag tortilla chips

1 package taco mix seasoning
1 green pepper, chopped
1 bunch scallions, chopped
1 can pitted black olives, drained and sliced

Mash avocados and place on large platter. Mix taco seasoning with sour cream and spread on avocados. Layer with green peppers, tomatoes, scallions and olives. Cover with cheese.

Serve with tortilla chips & enjoy!

[More...]

Stephen's Chicken Enchilada

Stuff a 3-5 pound chicken with an onion. Place in pot, cover with water. Add a few bay leaves and some peppercorns. Boil until chicken is cooked. Reserve chicken broth for enchilada sauce.

Enchilada Sauce

1 quart chicken broth
6 tablespoons chili powder
1 quarter teaspoon garlic
1 teaspoon cumin salt
salt & pepper to taste
2 tablespoons cornstarch whisked in 3 tablespoons hot water

Bring first 5 ingredients to a boil.
Whisk in cornstarch and boil 1 minute.

Filling

3 cups cooked chicken, shredded
3 quarters of a cup blanched almonds, sliced
1 quarter cup Monterey Jack cheese, shredded
1 medium onion, chopped
1 half cup enchilada sauce

Mix filling ingredients together.

Garnish

1 cup Monterey Jack cheese, shredded
6 scallions, chopped

12 Flour Tortillas

Dip tortillas in enchilada sauce,
put strip of filling across each one, and roll tightly.
Place side by side in pan, sprinkle with cheese.
Heat in oven at 350º for 10 minutes.
Spoon sauce over all, top with scallions,
and enjoy!

Stephen Merrill

GAZPACHO SOUP
Howard M. Metzenbaum
United States Senator, Ohio

"...Below is a favorite recipe of mine that is both 'Heart Smart' and fun."

3 cans tomato juice
1 cucumber - cut up fairly fine
1 green pepper - cut up fairly fine
1 clove garlic - mashed
2 tablespoons olive oil
1 tablespoon white wine vinegar
¼ tablespoon Tabasco sauce
½ cup ice water

Blend all of the above and keep in the refrigerator. Tastes better if made a day ahead. Serve with toppings of croutons, chopped eggs, etc. Season to taste. Serves 4.

Howard M. Metzenbaum

PASTA WITH SUNDRIED TOMATOES AND MUSHROOMS
Judith Michael
Author

*"Deceptions", "Possessions", "Private Affairs", "Inheritance",
"A Ruling Passion", "Sleeping Beauty", "Pot of Gold"*

*1 large onion, chopped
4 cloves garlic, peeled and minced
4 tablespoon extra virgin olive oil
½ cup sundried tomatoes (not in oil)
½ cup dried procini mushrooms
6 ounces fresh white mushrooms, chopped
1 teaspoon dried rosemary, crushed
salt and pepper
½ pound fettucine
Parmigiano cheese (optional)*

Cover sundried tomatoes and dried mushrooms with boiling water and let stand at least 40 minutes and up to several hours. Drain through cheesecloth, reserving liquid. Squeeze liquid from tomatoes and mushrooms with your hands and chop them coarsely.

Cook onion in olive oil over medium flame until golden; add garlic and cook one minute. Add reconstituted tomatoes and mushrooms; cook over low heat, stirring occasionally, for five minutes. Add fresh mushrooms and cook another five minutes, stirring occasionally. Add rosemary, salt and pepper, and ½ to ¾ cups of reserved soaking liquid. Cook over low heat for ten minutes, adding more liquid if the mixture gets too dry.

Boil fettucine until al dente; drain and place in large pasta serving dish; drizzle a little olive oil over it, then cover it with the tomato mixture. If desired, grate parmigiano cheese (use fresh only) over each serving. Serves 4.

Spicy Bay Recipe
CRAB CAKES
Barbara A. Mikulski
U.S. Senator from Maryland

1 pound crab meat
3 slices bread or 4 crackers
1 tablespoon dijon mustard
2 teaspoons Old Bay or Wye River seasoning
1 tablespoon mayonnaise (regular or light)
1 egg, beaten
1 tablespoon snipped parsley (optional)

PICK *over crab meat*. Remove crust from bread and break bread into small pieces. Mix bread with beaten egg. Add remaining ingredients. Form into cakes and sauté quickly in a small amount of fat. Cakes can also be broiled. Serves 6 people.

Barbara A. Mikulski

SILVER STATE POTATOES
Bob Miller
Governor, Nevada

4 medium potatoes, boiled, peeled, and grated
2 cups sour cream
1 tablespoon salt
1/4 cup milk
1/4 cup butter
1 regular can of Cream of Chicken Soup
1/2 cup grated cheddar cheese
1/2 cup chopped onion

Combine all ingredients except potatoes. Simmer on low heat until cheese melts. Add potatoes. Place in lightly greased baking dish. Top with crushed corn flakes mixed with softened butter. Bake at 350° approximately 1 hour or until golden brown. Freezes and reheats very well.

Chocolate Nugget

One of Bob Miller's Favorites

6 ounces Nestles Chocolate Chips
1 egg
1/2 teaspoon vanilla
Dash of salt
3/4 cup milk

Mix ingredients and microwave on high for 2 minutes. Put in blender for 1 minute. Pour in little cups and refrigerate until set.

OVEN STEW
Walter D. Miller *and his wife* Pat
Governor, South Dakota

1 1/2 - 2 pounds stew meat
3 large potatoes, chunked
4 stalks celery, chunked
4 carrots, chunked
1 large onion
raw mushrooms (optional)
1/2 cup tomato juice
1 tablespoon brown sugar
2 tablespoons tapioca
2 tablespoons salt
dash of pepper

Place meat and vegetables in 9 x 13 pan.

Mix rest of ingredients and pour over meat and vegetables.

Cover with foil and bake at 275º-300º, depending on oven, for 4 hours.

4 - 6 Servings.

PEACH COBBLER
Zell Miller
Governor, Georgia

3/4 cup flour
3/4 cup milk
pinch of salt
1 cup sugar
2 teaspoons baking powder
1/2 cup butter (melted)
2 cups fresh peaches (sliced)
1/2 cup sugar

Sift flour, salt, and baking powder .Mix in 1 cup sugar. Stir in milk and beat. Pour this batter over the melted butter.

Do not stir .

Pour peaches mixed with 1/2 cup sugar over this.

Do not stir .

Bake 1 hour at 350º.

Serves 4 - 6.

IRISH POTATOES
Thomas Monaghan, President
Domino's Pizza, Inc.

1 ½ pounds bacon
16 ounces fresh mushrooms, sliced
2 large onions, chopped
6 ounces almonds, slivered
4 to 5 potatoes, sliced
green onions, chopped
parsley, chopped
salt and pepper to taste

Fry bacon until crisp; drain, reserving grease. Sauté mushrooms, onions, and almonds in 2 tablespoons reserved grease; remove from skillet.

Fry potatoes until crisp in remaining grease. Combine sautéed mushroom mixture, potatoes, and remaining ingredients; toss well. Serve immediately. Makes 8 servings.

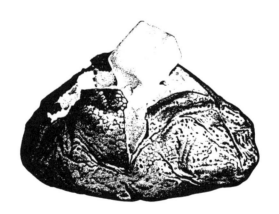

SAUTÉED TROUT WITH FRESH TARRAGON
Daniel Patrick Moynihan
U.S. Senator, New York

2 small brook trout, gutted, washed, and dried with paper towels
4 tablespoons butter
fresh tarragon leaves (generous handful), roughly cut
salt and pepper to taste
juice of 1 lemon

In a frying pan large enough to hold both fish, melt butter until nut brown in color (carefully watch so it does not burn). Add fish, tarragon, seasonings, and lemon juice. Cook on one side for about 3½ minutes. Turn trout gently with two wooden spatulas and continue to cook for about 4-5 minutes or until springy when touched and fork shows flesh is flaky.

Remove fish from pan and insert a sharp knife at the back of the trout's head, run knife along the back and underside and the whole bone will be exposed. Lift tail and it will come off intact with the head.   Place fillets on plates and divide sauce from pan. Serves 2.

POTATO DILL SOUP

7 large potatoes	*2 onions, chopped*
bunch of scallions, chopped	*large amount of fresh dill*
2 tablespoons butter	*1 pint heavy cream*
2 cups sour cream	*fresh ground black pepper*
salt to taste	*parsley for garnish*

Peel potatoes, cook with onions in boiling water until they begin to fall apart. Strain.

Add scallions, dill, butter, heavy cream and cook ten minutes. Stir in 1 cup sour cream and let it heat through for two minutes.

Garnish each bowl with pepper, dill, parsley and 1 teaspoon sour cream.

SWEDISH PANCAKES
Patty Murray
United States Senator, Washington

3 large eggs or 4 smaller eggs
1 scant teaspoon salt
3 teaspoons sugar
2 cups milk
1 1/2 cups flour
1 tablespoon butter, melted

Combine the flour, salt, and sugar in a bowl. Whip the eggs and milk together, then blend slowly into the dry mixture. Add the melted butter.

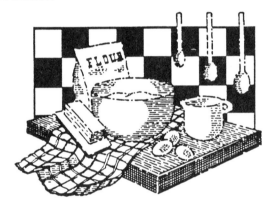

For one large pancake...

Pour the batter into a greased 12" cast iron skillet and bake in a pre-heated 350° oven until brown. Serve sprinkled with lemon juice, powdered sugar, and fresh fruit such as strawberries.

For individual pancakes...

Use a scant half cup of batter per pancake and fry in a greased skillet. These will be very thin and can be rolled. They can also be sprinkled with lemon juice and powdered sugar, and served with fresh fruit.

POTATO CASSEROLE
E. Benjamin Nelson
Governor, Nebraska

2 pounds frozen hash brown potatoes
1 teaspoon salt
½ cup onion, chopped
½ cup cream of potato soup
     or cream of chicken soup
2 cups grated cheddar cheese

½ cup melted butter
¼ teaspoon pepper
1 pint sour
    cream with chives
½ cup celery
    chopped

Defrost potatoes. Combine melted butter, salt, pepper, soup, and sour cream. Mix hash browns with onion, celery, and cheese. Mix in soup mixture. Pour into a greased 9" x 12" casserole dish. Serves 16.

Topping: 2 cups crushed potato chips
               ½ cup melted butter

Mix butter and chips. Sprinkle on top of casserole. Bake 45 minutes at 350°. This dish can be frozen and heated before serving.

AMBROSIA FRUIT & NUT MOLD

2 3-ounce packages of lime jello
1 small jar maraschino cherries, chopped
1 small can crushed pineapple, undrained

2 ½ cups boiling water
1 pint sour cream
½ cup walnuts

Dissolve jello in water. Set aside; when thoroughly cooled, add sour cream and mix well with mixer on slowest speed. Fold in rest of ingredients. Pour into greased mold and refrigerate for one hour. When ready to serve, place mold in pan of warm water briefly to loosen and then turn into a serving dish.

[More...]

COCONUT CAKE

1 package yellow cake mix
1 can Eagle Brand sweetened condensed milk
1 can cream of coconut
1 carton whipping cream, whipped

Bake cake according to package directions in a 9 x 12" pan. When it is done, poke holes in cake with a fork. Pour the can of condensed milk and can of cream of coconut over the cake. Let cool. Spread the whipped cream over the cake, then sprinkle with coconut flakes.

CHIP DIP

1 can shrimp - drained & rinsed
8 ounces cream cheese, softened
¼ cup chopped onion

½ cup chili sauce
½ cup mayonnaise
2 teaspoons horseradish

Blend chili sauce into cream cheese. Mix in rest of ingredients. Add shrimp carefully. Chill until ready to serve.

BAKED BEANS

3 pounds Italian sausage
2 large onions, chopped
2 large green peppers, cut into rings
3 large cans Van Kamp Pork & Beans, drained
2 teaspoons liquid smoke
3 12-ounces bottles chili sauce
32 ounce jar of molasses (use ⅔ of it)
4 teaspoons horseradish
3 teaspoons prepared mustard

Cut up sausage into small chunks and cook until brown. Remove from pan and add chopped onion. Cook onion until transparent. Mix sausage and onion with remaining ingredients with the exception of green pepper rings. Pour mixture into a 3 quart casserole dish. Arrange green pepper rings on top. Bake at 350° for 1½ hours.

A COLLECTION OF *PREFERRED* RECIPES
Don Nickles
U. S. Senator, Oklahoma

Crock-pot Cornish Hens

Wash and pat dry 3 Cornish hens. Prepare 8 oz. cornbread stuffing mix as directed and stuff hens.

¼ cup melted butter
2 tablespoons brown sugar
2 tablespoons lime juice
2 tablespoons Dry white wine
2 teaspoons soy sauce

Brush on hens and baste while cooking.

CORN, CHEESE, AND CHILE PIE

3 large eggs
1 cup sour cream
4 ounces Monterey Jack
1 can (8 ounces) cream corn (cut in ½" cubes)
1 can diced green chilies, drained
1 can (8 ounces) corn kernels, drained
½ teaspoon salt
1 stick butter, melted
½ cup yellow cornmeal
¼ teaspoons Worcestershire sauce
4 ounces sharp cheddar

Beat eggs in large bowl. Add remaining ingredients and stir well. Pour into well greased 9½" pie pan or quiche dish. Bake 350° for 1 hour. Let stand for 10 minutes before cutting.

[More...]

GARDEN SALAD

1 cup sugar
½ cup salad oil
½ teaspoon pepper
¼ cup vinegar
1 tablespoon green bean liquid   **Bring to boil and cool**.

Pour cooled liquid over the following:

1 can LeSeuer peas, drained
1 can white shoe peg corn, drained
1 can french style green beans, drained
1 small jar pimento, finely chopped
½ to 1 cup celery, finely chopped
½ to 1 cup onion, finely chopped
½ to 1 cup green pepper, finely chopped

Mix together well and refrigerate.

KOLACHES

2 3-ounce packages cream cheese (whip with fork)
2 sticks butter
2 cups flour - add one at a time

Mix well and knead up into a ball. Refrigerate 3-4 hours.

Cut up 4 cups apples - add cinnamon and a little sugar. Divide dough into fourths (each quarter will make 4 kolaches). Place apples in the middle of each square and fold up around it. Bake 20-25 minutes at 400º on ungreased cookie sheet.

GLAZE

1 cup powdered sugar
½ teaspoons vanilla
lemon extract
few drops of water

AUSTRALIAN MEAT PIE
Greg Norman
Golf Pro

1 ounce butter or margarine
2 small onions, finely chopped
2 pounds of chopped sirloin
2 tablespoons plain flour
2 1/2 cups beef bouillon or stock
salt and pepper to taste
1 teaspoon dried thyme
2 tablespoons Worcestershire sauce
1/4 cup chopped parsley
pinch nutmeg
pastry, store bought pastry works very well
1 egg, slightly beaten

Melt butter in a sauce pan. Add onions and fry over moderate heat until onions soften. Add beef and fry pressing down with fork until beef is browned, drain.

Sprinkle flour over beef, stir and continue cooking for a further 2 minutes. Remove pan from heat. Gradually add stock. Return pan to the heat and stir constantly until mixture boils and thickens. Add all remaining ingredients.

Cover pan and simmer over a low heat for 30 minutes. Line pie tin with pastry. Prick the base several times with a fork. Using a sharp knife trim off excess pastry. Spoon filling in. Brush around edge with beaten egg. Top with pastry pressing edges together. Cut a hole in center of pie. Brush with remaining egg.

Cook at 400° for 25 minutes or until crust is golden brown.

Serves 4 or 5.

DOUBLE CHOCOLATE BROWNIES
Sam Nunn
United States Senator, Georgia

3/4 cup all purpose flour
1/4 teaspoon baking soda
1/4 teaspoon salt
1 teaspoon vanilla
1/3 cup butter
2 eggs
2 tablespoons water
3/4 cup sugar
1/2 cup chopped pecans
1 12-ounce package semi-sweet chocolate chips

IN a small bowl, combine flour, baking soda, and salt. Set aside. In small saucepan, combine butter, sugar, and water; bring ***just to a boil***. Remove from heat. Add 6 ounces chocolate chips and vanilla. Stir until melted and mixture is smooth. Transfer to a large bowl. Add eggs, one at a time, beating after each addition. Gradually blend in flour mixture. Stir in remaining 6 ounces chocolate chips and nuts. Pour into greased 9-inch square baking pan. Bake at 350° for 40-45 minutes.

SHRIMP COCONUT & ORANGE SAUCE
Carroll O'Connor
Actor

24 medium size shrimp
1 pound dry shredded coconut
3 eggs
1 cup flour
1 quart peanut oil
some milk
salt & pepper to taste

Clean and de-vein shrimp, leaving tails. Mix eggs, flour, and enough milk to make a heavy dough, add salt & pepper. Lay coconut out on tray, dip shrimp into dough leaving tails clean, then roll shrimp in coconut and shake off excess. The above can be done in advance and refrigerated until ready to use later that day.

ORANGE SAUCE

2 (8 ounce) jars orange marmalade
1/4 cups dry sherry
2 tablespoons horseradish
few drops Tabasco

Put marmalade through blender, mix with sherry, horseradish and Tabasco to make a spicy orange sauce.

Just before serving,

Heat oil to 375°, fry shrimp about 3-4 minutes until coconut is golden brown, serve on bed of rice, garnish with orange slices, and serve sauce on the side.

Serves 4.

SUGARED BACON STRIPS
Arnold & Winnie Palmer
Golf Pro

BACON:

One-half to one pound depending on desired sweetness. Have at room temperature for best results.

BROWN SUGAR:

Approximately 1 cup.

*R*oll (or pat or shake) raw bacon in brown sugar and place strips on any flat pan with sides. Bake in a slow oven (275°-300°) for about 25-30 minutes until dark brown. You may turn over once with a pincher or tongs.

When bacon appears well done, remove with tongs and drain on brown paper very thoroughly (grocery bags are very good for this). As it cools, it will get hard and can then be broken into smaller pieces or served whole. This tedious chore can be done earlier in the day and stored in aluminum foil, then reheated to serve.

ZUCCHINI *RIPIENI*
Joe Paterno
Head Coach, Football - Penn State University

1 1/2 cups tomato sauce
4 medium sized zucchini
   scrubbed but not peeled
1/4 cup olive oil
1/2 cup finely chopped onions
12 teaspoon finely chopped garlic
1/2 pound ground beef chuck
1 egg, lightly beaten
2 ounces finely chopped prosciutto
   about 1/4 cup (optional)

1/2 cup fresh white bread crumbs
   (French or Italian bread)
6 tablespoons freshly grated
   imported Parmesan cheese
1/2 teaspoon dried oregano,
   crumbled
1 teaspoon salt
1/4 teaspoon freshly ground
   black pepper

*P*repare the tomato sauce *(your own special way)*. Preheat the oven to 375º. Cut the zucchini in half lengthwise and spoon out most of the pulp, leaving hollow boatlike shells about 1/4" thick. Set the shells aside and chop the pulp coarsely. Heat 3 tablespoons of olive oil in a heavy 8-10 inch skillet, add the onions and cook them over moderate heat for 8-10 minutes, or until they are soft and lightly colored. Add the zucchini pulp and the garlic and cook for about 5 minutes longer, stirring frequently. With a rubber spatula scrape the entire contents of the skillet into a large sieve set over a mixing bowl and let them drain.

> **Meanwhile**, heat a tablespoon of oil in the skillet, add the ground beef and brown it over moderate heat, stirring almost constantly with a large fork to break up any lumps. Scrape the beef into another sieve set over a bowl and let drain.

*N*ow, in a large mixing bowl combine the drained vegetables and meat.
Beat into them the lightly beaten egg, prosciutto, bread crumbs, 2 teaspoons of grated cheese, oregano, salt and pepper and taste for seasoning. Spoon this stuffing into the hollowed zucchini shells, mounding the top slightly. To bake the zucchini, use a 12x16 inch shallow baking dish into which 1 1/2 cups of tomato sauce have been poured. Then carefully arrange the stuffed zucchini on the sauce. Sprinkle their tops with 1/4 cup of cheese, dribble a few drops of olive oil over them and cover the dish tightly with aluminum foil. Bring the sauce to a simmer on top of the stove, then transfer the dish to the middle of the oven and bake the zucchini for 30 minutes, removing the foil after 20 minutes so that the tops of the zucchini can brown lightly. Serve directly from the baking dish.

[More...]

ORANGE CAKE

from Penn State University

1 large Florida orange
1 cup raisins
1/3 cup walnuts
1/2 cup vegetable shortening
1 cup sugar
2 large eggs
2 cups flour
1 teaspoon baking soda
1 teaspoon salt
1 cup milk

Squeeze 1/3 cup juice from orange; reserve for Orange-Nut Topping. Remove any seeds from orange; place unpeeled orange, raisins and nuts in blender or food processor; process until finely ground. Set aside. In large mixer bowl cream shortening and sugar; beat in eggs. Combine flour, baking soda and salt. Add to creamed mixture alternately with milk. Fold orange-raisin mixture into batter. Spread batter into a greased and floured 13x9x2 inch baking dish. Bake in preheated 350º oven 40 to 50 minutes. Cool 10 minutes.

ORANGE-NUT TOPPING

1/3 cup sugar
1/3 cup chopped walnuts
1 teaspoon ground cinnamon

Drizzle reserved 1/3 cup orange juice over warm cake. Combine sugar, walnuts and cinnamon; sprinkle over cake. Garnish with whole walnuts and orange slices, if desired. Serves 20.

FETTUCINE PRIMAVERA
Craig Patrick, General Manager
Pittsburgh Penguins

4 medium zucchini, sliced (3-4 cups)
2 cups small broccoli flowerlets
1/3 cup pine nuts
1/4 cup olive oil
1 tablespoon minced garlic
4 large tomatoes, skinned and chopped (about 4 cups)
1 cup snow pea pods, cut in half diagonally
1/4 teaspoon salt
1/4 teaspoon freshly ground black pepper
8-10 ounces fettucine, cooked al dente and drained
1/2 cup heavy cream (evaporated skim milk)
1 cup freshly grated Parmesan cheese
1/4 cup minced fresh basil or 1 teaspoon dried basil

Blanch zucchini in boiling water for 1 minute and drain. Blanch broccoli for 3-4 minutes in boiling water and drain. On cookie sheet, toast pine nuts about 2-3 minutes under broiler until light brown. In a large skillet heat olive oil. Add garlic, tomatoes, zucchini, broccoli, snow pea pods, salt, and pepper. Sauté briefly, about 2-3 minutes.

Add fettucine to skillet along with butter, cream, Parmesan, pine nuts, and basil. Toss gently and serve. Serves 6-8.

Sunday Morning
HAPPY PAPPY EGGS
Gregory Peck
Actor

8 eggs
4 slices good baked ham
1/3 cup chopped chives
1/3 cup cream or whole milk
2 or 3 pats of butter

Soft scramble the eggs in butter after mixing them with the milk or cream. Toss in the chives and the ham (cut into nickel size pieces). Don't let the eggs get hard. Keep the flame just below medium and stir gently with a long handled fork the whole time.

Don't overcook Happy Pappy Eggs.

When ready to eat, heap on the salsa and Tabasco as hot as you can stand it. Children may not favor the chives or the hot stuff. This is really a grown up recipe. It will serve four adults with or without hangovers. For those with hangovers, add a generous helping of home fried potatoes, black eyed peas, or chili and beans.

Start the whole procedure with a good Bloody Mary made with vodka and served in a large chilled glass.

Don't do this more than once a month or your cholesterol count will go through the roof.

SWEDISH LEMON ANGELS
PENN & TELLER
Illusionists - Comedians

1 egg
*1/2 cup buttermilk, **or***
1/4 cup milk mixed with 1/4 cup vinegar
1/2 teaspoon vanilla
5 teaspoons baking soda
1 cup lemon juice (fresh is best)
1 1/4 cups sugar
7/8 cup all purpose flour
8 tablespoons butter or margarine, melted

Preheat oven at 375º.

In a small bowl or 2-cup measuring cup, beat the egg until foamy. Add the buttermilk and the vanilla and blend well. Add the baking soda, **one teaspoon at a time**, sprinkling it in and beating until the mixture is smooth and the consistency of light cream. Add the lemon juice all at once and blend into the mixture. Stir, **do not beat** (you want it creamy but without a lot of air). The mixture will congeal into a pasty lump. Scoop it out of the bowl using a spatula and spread it on a floured surface. Sift the flour and 3/4 cup of sugar together and use the fingertips to work it into the egg-lemon mixture. With a floured rolling pin, roll the dough out 1/32" thick, and with the tip of a sharp knife, cut the **"angel"** shapes and twist up the edges to form a shell-like curve about 3/8" high. Sprinkle on the remainder of the sugar. Brush each "angel" with melted butter. Place angels one inch apart on an ungreased baking sheet and bake for 12 minutes or until golden.

If *you would like more information on Penn & Teller, feel free to write them, and include a SASE (self-addressed, stamped envelop), at:*

MOFO
P.O. Box 1196
New York, New York 10185-0010

STUFFED GREEN PEPPERS
From Lynda (Mrs. Richard) Petty
Car #43

1 1/2 pounds ground beef
1 medium onion, chopped fine
1 tablespoon chili powder
2 eggs
1 cup catsup
1 cup cornflakes
salt and pepper to taste
6 bell peppers cut in half and cleaned

Boil peppers 5 minutes. Mix other ingredients together. Stuff peppers with mixture and arrange in bottom of large Pyrex dish.

*S*auce:

2 1/2 cups catsup & tomato paste (use more catsup than paste)
2 tablespoons brown sugar
2 tablespoons ground mustard
1 tablespoon vinegar

Mix together. Pour sauce over peppers. Bake at 375° for 30 to 40 minutes.

TRIFLE *VICTORIA*
Victoria Principal
Actress - Director - Producer

2 packages frozen strawberries
2 packages Junkit brand Strawberry Danish dessert **or**,
1 6-ounce jar raspberry jam mixed with
nonfat vanilla yogurt
Approximately 2 cups orange juice
4 packages ladyfingers
3 packages vanilla pudding
1 package whole fresh strawberries, cleaned and stemmed

*T*haw the frozen strawberries. Drain the syrup, and put the berries in one bowl and the syrup in another.

If using the Danish dessert, combine it in a saucepan with the orange juice and the syrup from the strawberries instead of using water as called for in the directions on the box. Bring to a boil and cook for 1 minute. Add the thawed strawberries and set the pot aside to cool.

If using the jam and yogurt, mix together with the thawed strawberries and set aside.

Make the vanilla pudding as directed, and cool in a pan of cold water to keep a film from forming.

Line the bottom and sides of a large glass bowl (preferably with straight sides) with a layer of ladyfingers. Cover with a thin layer of vanilla pudding, then a thin layer of the strawberry mixture. Gently place successive layers of ladyfingers, pudding, and strawberry mixture, then another layer of ladyfingers, another of pudding, and a last, thick layer of the strawberry mixture. If you have any ladyfingers left, you can top with those. Arrange the fresh strawberries on top, and refrigerate until you are ready to serve.

ORIENTAL CHICKEN SALAD
David Pryor
U. S. Senator, Arkansas

"Due to the fact that I now must maintain a healthier diet,
as I urge everyone to do,
I am enclosing a recipe for Oriental Chicken Salad."

Salad:
1 large head of romaine lettuce-chopped
3 bunches of watercress-chopped
1 bunch scallions-sliced
1 can water chestnuts-sliced
6 ounces beansprouts, fresh if possible
3 stalks of celery-sliced

Garnish:
12 each cucumber slices
6 ounces julienne carrot
6 each large mushrooms-sliced
6 each radish rose

Dressing:
6 ounces olive oil
6 ounces low sodium soy sauce
dash of cinnamon

Also:
1 large roasting chicken breast

Poach or steam chicken breast until done. (Poaching liquid can be saved for a soup or sauce.) After cooling, de-bone chicken and shred using your fingers or a fork. Mix watercress, scallions, water chestnuts, bean sprouts, celery, and half of the chicken together. Toss with 1/2 of the dressing. Place romaine lettuce on plates or large bowls. Divide above mixture between bowls. Arrange two cucumber slices, 1 ounce of julienne carrot, 1 mushroom, 1 radish rose, and the rest of the chicken on top of the salad. Serve remaining dressing on the side.

CHOCOLATE CHIP COOKIES
Marc Racicot
Governor, Montana

1 1/2 cup Crisco
1/2 cup margarine
1 1/2 cup brown sugar
3/4 cup white sugar
1 1/2 teaspoons vanilla
3 eggs
3 1/4 cups flour + 2 tablespoons
1 1/2 teaspoons salt
1 1/2 teaspoons soda
1 1/2 large packages of chocolate chips

Mix and Bake at 350º for 10-12 minutes.

MUD PIE

First Layer: *35 Oreos crushed. Mix with 1/3 cup melted margarine. Freeze.*

Second Layer: *1/2 Gallon ice cream softened a little (can mix Sussie Mocha Coffee mix, 5-6 teaspoons.) Layer on top of crumb mixture. Freeze.*

Third Layer: *1 can Hershey's Hot Fudge Topping. Warm a little and spread on ice cream. Freeze 15 minutes.*

Fourth Layer: *1 4-ounce carton Cool Whip. Spread on top of chocolate. (Sprinkle almonds on top if desired.)*

POACHED EGGS IN SHERRY SAUCE
Prince Rainier III
Ruler of Monaco

6 eggs
1 cup Bechamel sauce
tomatoes
grated Swiss cheese
Back Canadian bacon
3 rounds of toast
1/4 cup sherry

Remove sauce from heat. Mix with 2 beaten yolks, half a cup of grated Swiss cheese, salt, pepper, and a quarter of a cup of sherry. Keep in double boiler.

Fry in butter 6 slices of tomato. Poach 6 eggs. Fry 6 slices of back Canadian bacon in butter. Butter 3 large rounds of toast and cut in halves.

Put on each half a slice of bacon, a fried slice of tomato, and a poached egg. Pour sauce, and decorate with watercress.

BAKED FRENCH TOAST
Sally Jessy Raphaël

As served at the Isaac Stover House
Owned by the Emmy Award-Winning TV Talk Show Host

1 loaf white bread cubed
8 ounces cream cheese cubed
8-12 eggs, depending on size
1/2 cup maple syrup
1 cup milk

Using a 11 x 13 inch pan, line the bottom with 1/2 of the bread cubes. Next, layer the cream cheese mixture on top of the bread. Then add the remaining bread cubes on top. Beat the eggs, maple syrup, and milk together. Pour entire mixture over bread. ***Cover and refrigerate overnight.***

Bake at 350° for 45 minutes or until lightly golden brown. Serves 8.

GROUNDNUT SOUP
Jerry Rawlings
President, Republic of Ghana

"In Ghana, soup is not a starter, but a main dish eaten with fufu (pounded plantain and cassava, or yam or cocoyam) or with rice or boiled yam."

REPUBLIC OF GHANA

1 1/2 pound cubed lamb, **or**
1 1/2 pound cubed beef, **or**
1 jointed chicken
1 large onion, chopped
3 large tomatoes
1 cup groundnut paste (peanut butter)
hot chile peppers to taste (or Tabasco)
salt
1 tablespoon cooking oil
water

Heat oil in large stewpan and lightly brown the meat. Add chopped onion. Before the onion browns, add water to cover the meat. Add the tomatoes, skinned, and liquidized. Add a few liquidized peppers. Allow to simmer until the meat is half-cooked.

Meanwhile, whisk the groundnut paste with one or two cups of water until it forms a milky liquid. Add the groundnut liquid to the pan and add salt to taste. Simmer until the meat is well cooked and the liquid has thickened and darkened slightly.

Optional
During the last few minutes of cooking, a few small whole okros (okra) and/or whole, parboiled and peeled garden eggs (small white egg-sized aubergines) may be added. Some people add shelled hard-boiled eggs to groundnut soup made with chicken.

"President Rawlings likes whole fresh chile peppers added (small round green ones, or the red or yellow "bonnet" type -- you could try jalapeños) but you should exercise caution! Even in Ghana where hot pepper goes into almost every dish, the President's soup makes most people gasp!"

Serve with rice, boiled white yam (if obtainable), or as a not very authentic substitute, boiled potatoes.

MONKEY BREAD
Nancy and Ronald Reagan

3/4 ounce yeast or 1 package dry yeast
1 to 1/4 cup milk
3 eggs
3 tablespoons sugar
1 teaspoon salt
3 1/2 cup flour
6 ounces butter, room temperature
1/2 pound melted butter
2 9-inch ring molds

In bowl, mix yeast with part of milk until dissolved. Add 2 eggs, beat. Mix in dry ingredients. Add remaining milk a little at a time, mixing thoroughly. Cut in butter until blended. Knead dough, let rise 1 to 1 1/2 hours until double in size. Knead again, let rise 40 minutes.

Roll dough onto floured board, shape into a log. Cut log into 28 pieces of equal size. Shape each piece of dough into ball, roll in melted butter. Use half of the pieces in each of buttered, floured molds. Place 7 balls in each mold, leaving space between. Place remaining balls on top, spacing evenly. Let dough rise in mold. Brush tops with remaining egg. Bake in preheated oven at 375° until golden brown, approximately 15 minutes.

LEMON CHICKEN
Harry Reid
U. S. Senator, Nevada

1 egg
6 or 8 boned chicken breasts seasoned bread crumbs
1 stick margarine
3 cloves garlic, minced
2 lemons (about 3/4 cup juice)
1 cup white wine (not cooking wine)
2 chicken bouillon cubes
12 ounces fresh mushrooms thickly sliced
1 pound linguini (spinach flavor goes well)

Dip chicken breasts in egg and then bread crumbs. Set aside.

Melt 1/4 stick of margarine in a pan. Add minced garlic and cook 'til brown (approximately 1 minute.) In same pan, brown chicken breasts on both sides. After browning, squeeze 1/2 the lemon juice on both sides of chicken breasts. Set aside in casserole dish.

In same pan used to brown chicken, melt rest of margarine (3/4 stick). Add wine, bouillon, remaining lemon juice, and mushrooms. Simmer 7-10 minutes.

Pour sauce and mushrooms over chicken. Cover casserole dish tightly and bake at 350º for 30-40 minutes.

15 minutes before done, boil water and cook linguini.

Serve chicken over pasta. Garnish with lemon peels.

Southwestern Pilaf
Ann W. Richards
Governor, Texas

1 cup Texmati white rice
1 cup Texmati brown rice
1 cup wheat berries
1 1/2 cups black beans
2 ounce pork salt
1 onion
2 garlic cloves

2 tablespoons olive oil
1 1/2 cups celery (diced fine)
1 1/2 cups onion (diced fine)
2 teaspoons garlic powder
2 teaspoons white pepper
2 teaspoons cumin
salt to taste

Cook white and brown rice in 3 3/4 cups of water until done (about 25 minutes). Simmer covered...don't overcook...no salt. Rinse in cold water. Drain well.

Cook wheat berries in 4 cups of water until done (about 1 1/2 hours). Rinse in cold water and drain well.

Cook black beans in 4 cups of water until done (not too soft).

Season water with salt pork, onion, and garlic cloves. When done, rinse in cold water.

Combine last 5 ingredients in 2nd column and sauté in olive oil until vegetables are translucent (about 5 minutes).

Fold all ingredients together. Salt to taste. Cover with foil and heat in 350° oven for 20-25 minutes.

Yield: (20) 1 cup servings (approximately).

BANANA PUDDING
Jeannie C. Riley
Country Music Star

1 can Eagle Brand Sweetened Condensed Milk
1 1/2 cups cold water
1 package (3.9 ounces size) instant vanilla pudding
2 cups whipping cream (whipped)
6 large bananas, sliced and dipped in
fresh lemon juice or, lemon concentrate
(May add Angel flake coconut)

In large bowl, combine milk and water. Add pudding mix and beat well. Chill in refrigerator for 5 minutes. Beat whipping cream. Add to pudding mixture by folding gently. In a large glass serving bowl pour 1/3 of pudding mix in bottom. Layer 2 times with bananas and vanilla wafers (if desired, coconut). End with pudding on top. *Garnish as you wish.*

"I love it."

Grandma's BROWN SUGAR ROLLS
Barbara Roberts
Governor, Oregon

"My Grandma Bessie Murray was a wonderful cook.
Although she seldom measured anything
with a standard measuring utensil, every dish
she prepared was a treat. This recipe is one of our family
favorites; however, I must admit
the sugar rolls always tasted better at Grandma's house when
we ate them for breakfast instead of toast."

Basic baking powder biscuit recipe:

"You might want to use a commercial biscuit mix;
however, Grandma would never have dreamed
of taking such a store-bought shortcut."

1 3/4 cup flour
1/3 cup shortening
2 1/2 teaspoons baking powder
3/4 teaspoon salt
approximately 3/4 cup milk

Blend dry ingredients and shortening until mixture resembles fine crumbs. Stir in just enough milk so that dough leaves sides of bowl and rounds into ball. Turn dough onto lightly floured surface and knead gently ten times.

Roll above or other biscuit dough out on lightly floured surface to 1/3 to 1/2 inch. Spread with butter or margarine and sprinkle with brown sugar. Roll up and cut into 1 inch slices. Place sliced rolls, cut side down, on lightly greased baking sheet or dish and bake at 350° for approximately 30 minutes or until lightly brown. Do not overcook.

"Grandma's rolls were always served hot and with lots of love. I
hope that you, too, enjoy serving
our family favorite the same way."

Barbara Roberts

CHICKEN CUTLETS ALA RUSSE
WITH PAPRIKA SAUCE
The Honorable & Mrs. John D. Rockefeller IV
U.S. Senator, West Virginia

2 large chicken breasts
1 tablespoon water
5 tablespoons melted butter
1/4 teaspoon nutmeg
6 tablespoons butter

1/2 cup all purpose flour
1 1/2 cups bread crumbs
1 large egg
1 teaspoon vegetable oil
salt and pepper

Chill your mixing bowl in freezer while you remove the skin and bones from the chicken breasts. Finely chop the chicken meat or put through a grinder using a fine blade. You should have 1 1/2 cups of ground meat. If your market has chopped chicken meat, you could save yourself the trouble. Turkey could also be substituted. Add the meat to the chilled bowl and add the nutmeg, salt and pepper to taste and the 5 tablespoons of melted butter. Beat well and chill in the freezer (do not freeze!). Season the 1/2 cup of flour with salt and pepper. Beat the egg with water in a small bowl and set aside. Take two pie pans and put the flour in one and the bread crumbs in the other. Now you have the three items lined up - flour, egg and bread crumbs. Have a piece of waxed paper next to the bread crumbs to put the dipped cutlet on. Divide the chicken into 8 balls and flatten to 1/2 inch thick. Shape into a cutlet. Dip each in the flour, then the egg, and finally into the bread crumbs. Press the crumbs into the meat gently. When all 8 cutlets are done place them into the refrigerator. At this time, make your Paprika Sauce and keep warm. The recipe for the sauce follows. In a heavy skillet, heat the 6 tablespoons of butter and 1 teaspoon of vegetable oil. When very hot carefully add the cutlets. Cook until golden brown on one side and turn and brown the other side. Arrange on a hot platter and spoon some of the Paprika Sauce over the cutlets and keep hot or serve immediately.
Serves 8.

PAPRIKA SAUCE

3 tablespoons butter
3 medium tomatoes
1/4 cup all purpose flour
3 tablespoons onion, finely chopped

2 tablespoons sour cream
salt and pepper
1 tablespoon Paprika

Peel the tomatoes and coarsely chop. You should have approximately 3 1/2 cups. Finely chop the onion for 3 tablespoons. Melt 2 tablespoons of butter in a skillet. Add onion and simmer until transparent and soft, do not brown. Stir in flour and Paprika, then stir in the tomatoes and add salt and pepper. Simmer 15 minutes, stirring frequently. Stir in the sour cream. Swirl in the remaining butter by rotating the pan gently. Taste and correct with salt and pepper. Serve hot.

[More...]

FANCY PEANUT SOUP

1 1/2 cups peanut butter
1 onion, chopped
1/2 teaspoon vegetable seasoning
2 celery ribs, chopped
1 quart chicken stock
3 tablespoons flour
3 tablespoons butter
1/2 teaspoon salt
1/2 cup peanuts, chopped
freshly ground pepper
1 quart milk

In a pan, over low heat, soften the peanut butter to allow for easy mixing with the milk. Add the milk, salt, pepper, and vegetable seasoning mixture. Bring to a boil and then set aside. Sauté the onion and celery in butter - do not allow to brown. Stir in the flour, as if making a gravy. Add the chicken stock and stir constantly until the mixture comes to a boil. It saves a lot of time and elbow grease if the stock has already been brought to a boil. Remove from the heat. Combine with the peanut butter and milk mixture. Return to the stove and over a very low heat, cook until all the ingredients are well blended. The soup may be served either hot or cold. After ladling the soup into individual soup bowls, sprinkle the chopped peanuts over the top for decoration. Serves 12.

FIRE AND *ICE* CHILI
Kenny Rogers
Country Music Star

"Dear Friends,

Good food shared with family and friends is one of the real pleasures in life. I'm on the road so much performing, recording or filming. It's really a treat to sit down and enjoy a relaxing meal. I'm pleased to share this recipe with you, it is a favorite of mine and believe me -- it is meant to warm a southern boy's heart and soul!"

Photo by Kelly Junkermann

1 can (20 ounces) pineapple chunks in syrup
1/4 cup chili powder
1 can (28 ounces) whole tomatoes, with juice
4 teaspoons ground cumin
1 can (6 ounces) tomato paste
1 tablespoon diced jalapeño chilies
1 can (4 ounces) diced green chilies
2 teaspoons salt
3 cloves garlic, pressed or minced
2 tablespoons olive oil
2 medium-size yellow onions, chopped
2 pounds lean boneless pork butt, cut into 1 inch cubes
1 green bell pepper, seeded and chopped cut into 1-inch cubes

Condiments: *small bowls of sliced green onions*
shredded cheddar cheese
dairy sour cream

Drain pineapple, reserving syrup. Drain and chop tomatoes, reserving juice. In large bowl, combine reserved syrup, tomatoes and juice, tomato paste, green chilies, 2 cloves garlic, 1 onion, bell pepper, chili powder, cumin, jalapeño chilies, and salt. Heat olive oil in Dutch oven until very hot. Brown pork on all sides in batches. (Don't overcrowd pot. Add just enough pork to cover bottom.) With all browned pork in pot, add remaining garlic and onion. Cook until onion is soft. Add tomato mixture to pork mixture. Cover and simmer 3 hours, stirring occasionally. Add pineapple for the last 30 minutes of cooking. Serve with condiments. Serves 8-10.

***For more fire**, add 2 tablespoons jalapeño chilies.*

"Happy Eating"

BEST APPLE PIE
Roy Romer
Governor, Colorado

2 1/2 pounds of cooking apples, pared, quartered,
   cored and thinly sliced (8 cups)
1/3 cup firmly packed light brown sugar
1/3 cup granulated sugar
1 tablespoon cornstarch **or**, 2 tablespoons flour
1/4 teaspoon ground cinnamon
1/4 teaspoon ground nutmeg
2 tablespoons butter or margarine
water or milk
sugar for sprinkling

*P*lace apples in large bowl. Mix sugars, cornstarch or flour, cinnamon, nutmeg, and salt in a small bowl. Sprinkle over apples; toss gently to mix. Let stand until a little juice forms, about ten minutes.

Meanwhile, prepare pie crust mix following label directions. Roll out half of dough to 12-inch round on lightly floured surface. Fit into 9-inch pie plate. Trim overhang to 1/2 inch.

*R*oll out remaining pastry for top to 12-inch round; fold into quarters, make 3 slits near center in each folded edge for steam to escape. Pile apple mixture into pastry and dot with butter or margarine. Moisten edge of bottom pastry with water. Place folded pastry on apples so point is on center; unfold. Trim overhang to 1 inch. Turn edges under and press together to seal. Pinch to make stand-up edge; flute.

For a crispy-sugary top, brush top of pastry with a little water or milk and sprinkle lightly with sugar.

*B*ake pie in hot oven (425°) for 40 minutes or until juices bubble through slits and apples are tender. If edges are browning too fast, cover with a narrow strip of foil. Cool for about an hour and serve with vanilla ice cream.

BAKED SHAD AND ROE
William V. Roth, Jr.
U.S. Senator, Delaware

1 medium to large shad, split
1 set - Shad roe
1/2 pint sour cream
paprika
lemon slices

Place the fish in a shallow baking dish, skin side down. Lay a piece of roe on each piece of fish. Cover the fish and roe with a thick layer of sour cream. Sprinkle with paprika. Put two thin lemon slices on each piece of fish. Bake 30 minutes at 400°.

MARY'S BEST LEMON PIE
James Sasser
U.S. Senator, Tennessee

1 1/2 cups plus 2 tablespoons sugar
1 tablespoon grated lemon rind
1/4 teaspoon cream of tartar
3 tablespoons lemon juice

4 eggs, separated
2 cups heavy cream
Butter for the pie pan

Sift together 1 cup of the sugar and the cream of tartar. Beat egg whites until stiff. Slowly fold in sugar mixture and beat until well blended. Butter the bottom and sides of a 9-inch pie plate. Scrape the meringue mixture into the pie plate, building it up around the edges to fashion a shell. Place in a pre-heated 275° oven and bake 1 hour. Remove and place on rack to cool. Beat egg yolks until light and lemon colored. Add 1/2 cup of the sugar. Add lemon rind and lemon juice and beat to blend. Cook in the top of a double boiler until thickened, stirring constantly. Remove from heat and let cool. Whip half of the cream until stiff and fold into the lemon filling. Pour this into the meringue shell. Chill until the filling is set. Whip the remaining cream with the remaining 2 tablespoons of sugar and spoon on top of the filling. Chill, uncovered for 24 hours.

Mary's Bran Muffins

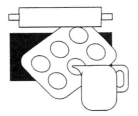

2 cups bran (not bran cereal)
1 cup raisins
2 cups sifted flour
1 cup buttermilk
2 teaspoons baking soda
3 tablespoons dark molasses
1/4 teaspoon salt
1/2 cup vegetable oil
3/4 cup sugar
1 large egg, at room temperature

Lightly coat with nonstick cooking spray the insides of muffin tins (1-1/2" deep) to accommodate about 15 muffins. Thoroughly blend together the bran, flour, baking soda, salt, sugar, and raisins in a bowl. Whisk the buttermilk, molasses, oil, and egg in a bowl, pour over dry ingredients and mix until well blended. Fill each cup 3/4 full of batter and bake muffins on the middle level rack at 325° for 20 to 25 minutes or until a wooden pick inserted in the center withdraws cleanly. Cool the muffins in the pan for one minute, then remove to cooling racks.

ROASTED POTATO SKINS
WITH SCALLION DIP
Diane Sawyer, ABC News

4 pounds baking potatoes scrubbed well and patted dry
coarse salt to taste

With a paring knife, peel the skin from the potatoes lengthwise into 1/4 inch wide strips, removing a thin layer of the flesh with each strip. In a bowl of cold water, reserve the potatoes for another use, such as bacon and potato salad. Arrange the strips, skin side up in one layer in well buttered jelly-roll pans and bake them in a preheated 450° oven for 15 to 20 minutes or until they are crisp and golden.

TOSS the potato skins with the salt, transfer them to racks and let them cool. The potato skins may be made up to one day in advance, kept in an airtight container and served at room temperature or reheated in a preheated 450° oven for 5 minutes or until they are hot.

Scallion DIP
1 small garlic clove
1/4 cup chopped scallions
1/2 cup chopped fresh parsley leaves
1/2 cup sour cream
1/2 cup mayonnaise
1 teaspoon Worcestershire sauce or to taste

In a food processor or blender, mince the garlic, scallions and parsley, add the sour cream and mayonnaise. Blend the mixture until it is smooth. Blend in the Worcestershire sauce. Salt and pepper to taste. Transfer the mixture to a bowl and chill it, covered overnight to allow the flavors to develop. The dip may be made up to 3 days in advance and kept covered and chilled.

Serve the potato skins with the scallion dip. Serves 6 as an *hors d'oeuvre*.

SCHAEFER'S WAFERS
William Donald Schaefer
Governor, State of Maryland

"Maryland offers the best of many different worlds: the celebrated mountains of Western Maryland; the sandy, white beaches of Ocean City; the beauty of our Chesapeake Bay; and the many monuments and tributes to history that have been preserved and maintained throughout the State."

Beat 2 egg whites, which are at room temperature, until stiff.
Add 1/3 cup of sugar and beat 3 minutes.
Add another 1/3 cup of sugar and beat 3 minutes.
Add 1/2 teaspoon of vanilla.
Fold in one 6-ounce package of Toll House Chocolate chips.
Drop by teaspoon onto cookie sheet.
Place in oven preheated oven to 375°.
Count to ten, turn off oven.
Leave the cookies in the oven overnight.

Makes fifty.

CHEEZY CRAB HORS D'OEUVRES

1 cup (8 ounces) Maryland crab meat
1 (8 ounce) package cream cheese, softened
1 tablespoon instant minced onion
1/2 teaspoon horseradish
salt and pepper to taste
1 (2 ounce) package slivered almonds

Remove cartilage from crab meat. Blend together cream cheese, milk, onion, and horseradish. Gently mix in crab meat. Add salt and pepper. Put in shallow baking dish (1 quart), sprinkle with almonds. Bake at 350° until lightly browned on top, about 20 minutes. Serve hot on crackers or as a dip. Makes about 2 cups.

William Donald Schaefer

TOFFEE NUT BARS
Edward T. Schafer
Governor, State of North Dakota

1/2 cup shortening
1/2 cup brown sugar

Cream these ingredients together. Stir in:

1 cup regular flour

Press mixture down in a 9x13 inch greased pan. Bake at 350° for 10 minutes.

Beat

2 eggs well

Add

1 cup brown sugar
1 teaspoon vanilla

Beat well

Add

2 tablespoons flour
1 teaspoon baking powder
1 cup chopped nuts (either pecans or walnuts)
1 cup coconut

Spread over baked cookie-like mixture, then bake at 300° for an additional 25 minutes. Cut into bars and sprinkle with confectioners sugar and ***enjoy***.

CHEESE CAKE
Claudia Schiffer's
Model

the CRUST

1/2 to 3/4 cup of crushed crackers
melt 1 stick butter
1/2 cup of sugar

Mix everything together until blended. Put in a 10 inch pie plate and form with hand or a spoon then put into the fridge until the cheese is prepared.

the CHEESE

1 large & 1 small package of cream cheese

Beat until fluffy and add:

1/4 cup of sugar
1 healthy shake of salt
2 eggs at-a-time (high speed)
1 tablespoon of vanilla
1 tablespoon of lemon juice

Put the mixture into the pie crust. Put into the oven at 350° on middle rack for 25 minutes (or less).

the TOPPING

1 pint of sour cream

Mix:

2 tablespoons of sugar
1 tablespoon of vanilla

Spread on pie after 25 minutes. Bake for 10 minutes more. After cooling, cover with pie fillings red or black fruit.

RED VELVET CAKE
Willard Scott
Weatherman - TV Personality

"...pleasing to the palate"

1 1/2 cups sugar
2 ounces red food coloring
2 tablespoons cocoa
1 cup buttermilk
2 1/4 cups flour
1 teaspoon vanilla

1 teaspoon salt
1 teaspoon baking soda
2 eggs
1 tablespoon vinegar
1/2 cup shortening

Cream shortening with sugar, add eggs and beat well. Make a paste of cocoa and food coloring. Add to creamed mixture. Sift flour and salt <u>twice</u>. Add buttermilk alternately with flour to creamed mixture. Add vanilla. Put vinegar in deep bowl, add soda (it will foam). When blended, add to creamed cake batter. Do not beat batter, just blend well.

Grease and flour two 9-inch cake pans; pour batter into pans and bake at 350° for 25-30 minutes.

CREAM CHEESE FROSTING

8 ounces light cream cheese, room temperature
5 tablespoons unsweetened pineapple juice concentrate
1/2 teaspoon vanilla extract
1/2 teaspoon finely grated orange zest

Place ingredients in bowl, whisk together until smooth. Good on Red Velvet Cake.

TABOULEH
Donna Shalala, Secretary
U.S. Department of
Health and Human Services

3 bunches of parsley (de-stemmed) (3 cups chopped fine)
2 bunches of mint (preferably the tips, also de-stemmed)
  (2 cups chopped fine)
1 small bunch of scallions (1/2 cup)
3/4 cup lemon juice (squeezed from several large lemons)
2 cups chopped ripe tomatoes (for color)
1/2 cups cracked wheat (fine or medium bulgur)
salt and pepper
1/4 cup virgin olive oil

Soak the cracked wheat in water and lemon juice to cover for 3 hours. Meanwhile, wash and dry parsley and mint well. Chop parsley fine. Chop mint separately. Slice scallions. Cut tomatoes in small pieces.

Drain cracked wheat - squeezing out juice. Combine wheat with other ingredients and mix well. Season to taste with salt and pepper and more lemon juice and a small amount of olive oil.

Try to wait before eating until flavor melds. Eat with lettuce leaves, young grape leaves, or thin Lebanese bread.

Secretary Shalala's
Golden Retriever "Bucky"
loves Tabouleh for a special treat.

DOVE ON THE GRILL
Richard Shelby
Governor, Alabama

Dove (allow at least 2 per person)
salt, pepper, and Worcestershire sauce to taste
bacon (1/2 slice per bird)

Sprinkle dove with salt, pepper, and Worcestershire. Wrap each dove with bacon. Secure with toothpick if necessary. Cook over a medium fire until done, about 20-30 minutes. Turn occasionally.

Variation

Wrap 1/2 strip of bacon around a water chestnut and a boneless dove breast. Season lemon butter with Worcestershire sauce and baste frequently. Cook on grill or broil until bacon is done.

"One of my favorite activities is hunting. This is a simple yet delicious way to prepare wild dove."

Richard Shelby

LEMON MOUSSE
U.S. Senator and Mrs. Paul Simon
Illinois

Pour 2 cups boiling water over 6-ounce package of lemon jello and stir until dissolved. Add 2 7-ounce bottles of lemon lime carbonated drink (like 7-Up). Add grated rind of 1 lemon and juice. Chill until slightly thick (about 2 hours). Beat until foamy. Fold in 2 cups heavy cream (whipped). Turn into a 2-quart soufflé dish and chill until firm. Serve with fresh berries, slightly sweetened. This mousse serves 8.

CHEESE PIE

8 ounces package cream cheese, softened
1 unbaked, 8" graham cracker crust

1/2 cup sugar	2 eggs
1 tablespoon lemon juice	1 cup sour cream
1/2 teaspoon vanilla	1 tablespoon sugar

Beat cheese until fluffy. Gradually blend in 1/2 cup sugar, lemon juice, vanilla and dash of salt. Add eggs, one at a time, beating well. Pour filling into crust. Bake at 325° for 25-30 minutes, until set. Combine rest of ingredients and spoon over top of pie and bake 10 minutes longer. Chill.

Honey Whole Grain Bread

3 cups white flour
1/2 cup honey
2 packages active dry yeast
2 eggs
1 1/2 teaspoons salt
1 cup water
1 cup cottage cheese
4 tablespoons butter

2 1/2 cups whole wheat flour
1/2 cup regular rolled oats
2/3 cup chopped walnuts or pecans

In a large bowl, combine 2 cups white flour with yeast and salt. Heat water, cottage cheese, butter, and honey until very warm (120°-130°). Add warm liquid and eggs to flour mixture. Mix well. Add whole wheat flour, oats, and nuts. Stir in remaining white flour (add more if necessary). Knead until smooth and elastic. Let rise until double. Punch down and place in two greased 5 1/4 x 9 1/4 x 3 inch pans. Let rise about one hour. Bake at 350° for 35-40 minutes. Remove from pans onto cooling rack. Brush tops with butter.

Blender Cheesecake
Alan K. Simpson
U.S. Senator, Wyoming

*Senator Simpson submitted this on behalf of
his "lovely wife", Ann.
"It is a dandy and has always been one of my favorites."*

Preheat oven 350º

Crust:

*1 cup graham crackers (or 12 graham crackers)
1/2 stick melted butter*

Mix and press in pie plate.

Filling:

*4 3-ounce packages of cream cheese (softened)
2 eggs
3/4 cup sugar*

Blend well, till creamy. *"YOU CAN'T OVER BEAT."* Pour into crust. Bake at 350º for 20 minutes. Remove from oven and cool for 5 minutes.

Topping:

*1/2 pint sour cream
3 tablespoons sugar
1 teaspoon vanilla*

Mix and pour over cheesecake. Spread around. Put back in oven for 10 minutes, covered. Cool and refrigerate. Top with frozen strawberries. Serves 8-10.

CREME de MENTHE BROWNIES
Bob Smith
U.S. Senator, New Hampshire

"Sinfully chocolate! A St. Patrick's Day favorite - unbelievably delicious!" -- Mrs. Mary Jo Smith --

1 3/4 cups butter or margarine	1 cup flour
1 cup sugar	1/2 cup chopped nuts
2 cups (16 ounces) chocolate syrup	2 cups powdered sugar
4 eggs, beaten	3 tablespoons Creme de Menthe
1 teaspoon vanilla	1 cup chocolate chips

First Layer: Creme 1/2 cup butter with 1 cup sugar. Add chocolate syrup, beaten eggs, vanilla, flour and nuts. Pour into buttered 9 x 13 inch pan. Bake at 350° for 25 minutes. Cool.

Second Layer: Cream powdered sugar, 1/2 cup butter, and Creme de Menthe together. Spread on chocolate layer.

Third Layer: Melt chocolate chips and 3/4 cup butter. Cool slightly and spread on green layer, but don't swirl.

Cut and cool into squares.

SMITH FAMILY GINGERBREAD

"A very dark, molasses gingerbread. Moist and very special. And ah-h, the smell of your kitchen! "

Bob Smith

1 cup shortening or margarine	1 egg, well beaten
1 cup dark molasses	1 pinch of salt
1 cup sugar	2 teaspoons of ginger
2 1/4 cups of flour	
1 cup sour milk (milk with 1 tablespoon lemon juice or vinegar)	
1 teaspoon baking soda, dissolved in 2 teaspoons of boiling water	

Bring shortening, molasses, and sugar to a boil and set aside. Mix sour milk, beaten egg, baking soda, water, and salt together and add to molasses mixture. Sift flour and ginger together and add to original mixture. Bake for 45-60 minutes in a 300°-325° oven.

REFRIGERATOR STIR FRY
Dick Smothers
Entertainer

"This is my favorite way to make a delicious meal and use up leftover vegetables. I pull out all of the vegetables I have on hand, both fresh and leftover. It's a different combination of vegetables every time I make it. Be creative and experiment."

You will need a total of 4 cups of vegetables in any combination you prefer. Some of my favorites to choose from are:

peas	tomatoes	beans
broccoli	celery	carrots
corn	bell peppers	mushrooms
cauliflower		

SAUCE

1/3 cup canned chicken stock de-fatted
1 tablespoon soy sauce
1 tablespoon teriyaki sauce
1 teaspoon corn starch
2 teaspoons fresh grated ginger root (optional)

MIX all ingredients thoroughly and set aside

CHICKEN

Cut 3 chicken boneless breasts into 1 inch cubes
Chop 3 cloves garlic
Sauté chicken and garlic until done
Set aside

VEGETABLES

Coat wok/large skillet with vegetable oil & heat ;
Add 1/4 cup of canned chicken broth and 4 cups
of mixed vegetables cut into 1 inch cubes;
Stir fry vegetables 2-3 minutes, stirring constantly;
Add cooked CHICKEN and SAUCE;
Cook 2-3 minutes more, stirring constantly until liquid thickens.
Serve over brown rice or pasta.

"This feeds my family of 4."

GRILLED AVOCADO SWORDFISH
Tommy Smothers
Entertainer

"Our friend Marla Rowan shared this recipe with me, and it has since become my favorite dish! I can't remember all the measurements, so you figure it out."

fresh swordfish steaks, about 1 - 1 1/2" thick
red onion, minced
avocado, chopped in small chunks
fresh lemon juice
chopped cilantro
fresh garlic, minced

Marinade

I love Susan's Secret Sauce which is made in Sonoma. As an alternative mix together:

soy sauce (or for a sweeter taste, teriyaki sauce)
fresh minced garlic
lemon juice
a splash of Worcestershire sauce

Carefully cut a large pocket in the center of the swordfish with a sharp knife and set aside. Mix the avocado, onion, cilantro, lemon juice, and garlic in a bowl. Stuff the mixture into the swordfish, securing the end with toothpicks if necessary. Pour marinade over the top of fish and allow to sit in the refrigerator for a few hours.

Grill over hot coals 2 to 4 minutes on each side, until done, or burnt, whichever comes first.

A CARAMEL PINEAPPLE CAKE ROLL
Senator Arlen and Joan Specter
U.S. Senate, Pennsylvania

2 cans crushed pineapple, drained
1/2 cup dark brown sugar
3/4 cup cake flour
1 teaspoon baking powder
1/2 teaspoon salt
4 large eggs, separated
3/4 cup sugar
2 teaspoons vanilla
1 teaspoon grated lemon rind

BUTTER well a 10" x 15" jelly roll pan. Spread drained fruit evenly over bottom of pan and sprinkle with brown sugar. Sift flour with baking powder and salt. Beat egg whites until foamy and add 3/4 cup of white sugar gradually, beating until stiff.

BEAT yolks into stiffened whites, and add vanilla and lemon rind. Sprinkle flour over all and gently fold in. Spread batter evenly over the pineapple and brown sugar.

BAKE in a preheated oven at 375° for 18 to 20 minutes. Turn upside down on a damp towel and sprinkle lightly with confectioners sugar. Roll up in towel and cool. Remove towel when cool, place cake on platter and ice.

ICING

1 cup heavy cream
3 tablespoons confectioners sugar

Beat heavy cream with sugar until stiff.

FAVORITE RESTAURANTS
Gloria Steinem
Author - Activist

Jezebels
630 9th Avenue
New York City

Luma
200 9th Avenue
New York City

The Russian Tea Room
150 West 57th Street
New York City

POTATO GOULASH
Jan Stráký
Minister of Transport of the
Czech Republic

3 tablespoons of lard
1 big onion, finely chopped
2 Speckwursts (or sausage), cut into cubes
4 big potatoes, peeled and cubed
1.5 liter water
Salt, pepper, hot red pepper, goulash seasoning

Melt lard in a large saucepan, sauté onion until limp. Add red pepper and sausage. Cook for 5 minutes. Add water, potatoes, salt, and pepper. Boil for approximately 15 minutes. Add goulash seasoning at the end.

Best when served with bread and beer.

STUFFED ANGEL FOOD CAKE
Mike Sullivan
Governor, Wyoming

"...this is what Mike likes for his birthday..."

Angel food cake

Cut cake 1 inch from top, cut out one inch deep.

Filling & Icing

3 cups whipping cream (whip)
1 cup confectioners sugar
3/4 cups crushed pineapple (strained)
large carton strawberries
6 marshmallows cut in 1/4's

Mix above, use half for filling and rest for icing. Decorate top with strawberries.

Keep cake in refrigerator overnight to bring out flavor.

CHIPPED BEEF DIP
Bruce Sundlun
Governor, State of Rhode Island

2 tablespoons heavy cream
1 8-ounce package cream cheese
1 8-ounce package chopped chipped beef
1 tablespoon horseradish
1 medium onion, finely chopped
dash of Worcestershire sauce
rye crackers

Soften cream cheese with heavy cream. Add onion, horseradish, and Worcestershire sauce. Mix well. Shape into ball and wrap chipped beef around cheese ball and **CHILL**. Serve with rye crackers.

ANN & FIFE's LASAGNA
Fife Symington
Arizona State Governor

"Our recipe for lasagna is definitely a crowd pleaser..."

2 pounds extra lean ground beef
1 large onion, chopped
1 clove garlic, minced
6 bay leaves (remove after cooking)
salt and pepper
1 12-ounce can tomato paste
2 12-ounce cans of water

12 lasagna noodles
1 cup cottage cheese
1/4 cup Parmesan
  (freshly grated)
1/2 pound mozzarella
  (grated)

Cook above ingredients together slowly, at least one hour. 20 minutes before meat is done, cook twelve lasagna noodles as directed on package. Rinse in cold water, keep in water until ready to use. In a glass dish (16x11x2) place six noodles. On top of noodles put half of sauce, 1 cup cottage cheese, 1/4 cup fresh grated Parmesan cheese and 1/2 pound grated mozzarella cheese. Start with noodles and repeat. Cover with foil, place on cookie sheet and bake at 350° for 45 minutes. Let rest at least 20 minutes before serving. Serves 12.

TURKEY SOPA

"and the Turkey Sopa has a uniquely southwestern taste."

1 dozen corn tortillas cut into 1" strips
3 cups cooked turkey of chicken
1/2 stick butter or margarine
1 jar Old El Paso Taco Sauce
1 medium onion, chopped
1 can diced green chilies
1 can cream of mushroom soup
1 can cream of chicken soup
1 can consomme
1 pound jack cheese, shredded
1 pound cheddar cheese, shredded

Fife [signature]

Melt butter. Add onions. Cook until tender. Add green chilies, taco sauce, soup and turkey or chicken. Place layer of tortillas on bottom of 2 inch casserole. Place alternate layers of soup mixture, tortillas and cheese. Repeat for 3 layers, making sure top layer is cheese. Bake 30 minutes to 1 hour until thoroughly heated and cheese is melted at 350°. Serves 8-10.

SPICY CHICKEN
Elizabeth Taylor
Actress - Activist

2 teaspoons curry powder
1 teaspoon cumin
1/2 teaspoon ground ginger
1/2 teaspoon turmeric
1/2 clove garlic, crushed
1 onion, chopped
1 teaspoon fresh ginger, grated
1 medium chicken, cut into serving pieces and skinned

Combine dry ingredients with garlic, onion and fresh grated ginger. Coat chicken with mixture and refrigerate for 2 hours, preferably longer.

Place on moderately hot barbecue grill or broil in oven approximately 30 minutes or until done, turning once.

ISIAH's FAVORITE CHEESECAKE
Isiah Thomas
Former Detroit Pistons

Crust

1 3/4 cup graham cracker crumbs
1/4 cup ground walnuts
1/2 teaspoon cinnamon
1/2 cup melted butter

*M*ix all ingredients in a spring form pan and pat down on bottom.

Filling

3 beaten eggs
1 cup sugar
3 cups sour cream
2 8-ounce packages cream cheese (softened)
1/4 teaspoon salt
2 teaspoons vanilla extract
1/2 teaspoon almond extract

*B*lend all ingredients together in mixer. Pour in pan and bake at 300° for 50-60 minutes. Turn oven off and open door slightly.   Leave cake in oven an additional 40 minutes. Remove and refrigerate overnight.

DAVE's
OLD FASHION CHILI
R. David Thomas
Senior Chairman of the Board & Founder
Wendy's International, Inc.

2 pounds fresh ground beef
1 quart tomato juice
1 29-ounce can tomato purée
1 15-ounce can dark red kidney beans, drained
1 15-ounce can small red beans, drained
1 medium onion (1 1/2 cups), chopped
1/2 cup celery, diced
1/4 cup chili powder
2 teaspoons cumin
1 1/2 tablespoons garlic powder
1 teaspoon salt
1/2 teaspoon each of black pepper, oregano, sugar
1/8 teaspoon cayenne pepper

In frying pan, brown ground beef and drain. Add remaining ingredients and drained ground beef into 6 quart pot. Cover and simmer 1 to 1 1/2 hours, stirring every 15 minutes. Yields 16 8-ounce servings.

Dave

**Dave likes to add fresh,
chopped onions on top of his chili serving!**

BROCCOLI & CHEESE QUICHE
Tommy G. Thompson, Governor
Wisconsin

pastry for 10-inch single pie crust
1 1/2 cups grated cheddar cheese
1 1/2 cups cream
dash of pepper

1 1/2 cups chopped broccoli
4 eggs
1/4 teaspoon salt
dash of nutmeg

Arrange broccoli and cheese in pastry-lined pan. Beat together eggs, cream, and spices in bowl. Pour the custard mixture over cheese and broccoli. Place in preheated oven at 375° for 35-40 minutes or until top is golden brown and knife inserted 1 inch from edge comes out clean. 8 main dish servings.

Joe Dodge, Chef, Executive Residence Kitchen

BLUEBERRY BUCKLE

Mrs. Thompson's Favorite!

2 cups sifted flour
1/2 teaspoon salt
2 teaspoons baking powder
1 cups fresh or frozen blueberries

1 egg
1/4 cup soft butter
1 cup sugar
1/2 cup milk

Sift together flour, baking powder, and salt. Cream butter and sugar until light and fluffy. Add the egg and milk and beat well. Add the flour, baking powder, and salt and stir until blended. Add blueberries. Spread mixture into 9x13 inch pan.

1/2 cup brown sugar
1/3 cup flour
1/4 cup soft butter
1/2 teaspoon cinnamon

Topping

Cream together butter and sugar. Combine flour and cinnamon and add to creamed mixture. Stir until crumbly. Sprinkle over blueberry buckle and bake 35-45 minutes at 350°.

South Carolina PECAN PIE
Strom Thurmond
U.S. Senator, South Carolina

3 eggs
1 cup dark brown sugar
1 cup light corn syrup
1 tablespoon melted oleo

1/8 teaspoon salt
1 teaspoon vanilla extract
1 cup pecans, chopped
9 inch pastry shell

Beat eggs, adding sugar gradually; add syrup, oleo, salt, vanilla, and pecans. Pour into pastry shell. Bake at 360° for 1 hour.

MINIATURE HAM ROLLS

2 packages of small tea rolls
6 ounces Swiss cheese slices
1/2 teaspoon Worcestershire sauce
1 tablespoon onion flakes

8 ounces of sliced ham
1 1/2 tablespoons mustard
1 1/2 teaspoon poppy seed

Slice rolls lengthwise through center. Put ham and cheese on bottom. Put roll top back on. Mix remaining ingredients and pour over top. Cover with foil and bake for 15 minutes at 350°. Rolls can be frozen.

LIB'S SWEET POTATO CASSEROLE
Randy Travis
Country Music Star

3 cups cooked, mashed sweet potatoes
1 cup sugar
2 eggs
1 teaspoon vanilla
1/2 cup butter or margarine
1/3 cup milk

TOPPING

1 cup firmly packed brown sugar
1/3 cup all-purpose flour
1/3 cup butter or margarine
1 cup finely chopped pecans

Combine sweet potatoes, sugar, eggs, vanilla, milk, and 1/2 cup butter. Beat with electric mixer until smooth. Spoon into a greased 2 quart shallow casserole.

Combine brown sugar, flour, 1/3 cup butter, and pecans. Sprinkle over top of casserole.

Bake at 350° for 30 minutes.

Yields 8 to 10 servings.

GRANDMA'S BEEF STROGANOFF
Jim Guy Tucker
Governor, Arkansas

2 pounds filet of beef
1 cup chopped onion
3 tablespoons flour
1 tablespoon catsup
1/8 teaspoon pepper
1/4 cup dry white wine
1 1/2 cup sour cream
1 1/2 cup cooked white rice
   or 3 cups cooked noodles

4 tablespoons butter
1 clove garlic, finely chopped
2 teaspoons meat extract paste
1/2 teaspoon salt
1 can beef bouillon, undiluted
1 tablespoon fresh snipped dill
1 1/2 cup cooked wild rice

*T*rim fat from beef and cut filet crosswise into 1/2 inch thick slices. Cut each slice across grain into 1/2 inch wide strips (about 2 inches long). Slowly heat large heavy skillet. Melt 1 tablespoon butter, add beef strips, just enough to cover skillet bottom. Over high heat sear quickly on all sides. Remove with tongs as meat finishes browning (it should be brown on outside and rare inside). In 3 tablespoons hot butter in same skillet, sauté onions, garlic and mushrooms until onion is golden (about 5 minutes). Remove from heat, add flour, meat extract paste, catsup, salt and pepper. Stir until smooth. Gradually add bouillon, bring it to a boil, stirring. Reduce heat and simmer 5 minutes. Over low heat add wine, the snipped fresh dill or dried dill and sour cream stirring until well combined. Add beef and simmer until sauce and beef are hot. Lightly toss wild and white rice.

Surround stroganoff with rice. Snip dill or parsley on top.

Chocolate Sour Cream Cake

*C*ream together: 2 cups sugar   1 cup Crisco   1/2 cup cocoa

*A*dd: 2 eggs

*A*dd alternately: 1 carton sour cream   2 1/2 cups flour
    2 teaspoons soda   1 teaspoon salt

*A*dd: 1 cup boiling water   2 teaspoons vanilla

Bake one hour at 350°.

STEAK AND SAUERKRAUT ROLLS
George V. Voinovich
Governor, Ohio

3 pounds flip steaks (or round steak pounded thin)
1/2 pound bacon
1 can sauerkraut (drained; reserve juice)
flour

On each steak lay 1/2 slice bacon. Put small mound of sauerkraut on top; roll tightly. Tie with string or secure with toothpicks. Roll in flour and brown quickly in approximately 1/2 cup hot fat. Remove meat.

1 beef bouillon cube dissolved in 2 cups boiling water
3/4 cup boiling water
2 tablespoons salt
1/2 teaspoon pepper
1/2 teaspoon Accent

Pour hot bouillon into roaster; add meat. Drain off fat from frying pan. Add 3/4 cups boiling water to pan, stir to mix in particles of browned flour. Pour liquid over meat along with sauerkraut juice; add seasonings. Cover roaster. Bake 2 hours at 325°. Makes about 20 rolls.

ONO BANANA BREAD
Governor John and Lynn Waihee
HAWAII

2 cups sifted flour
3/4 teaspoon salt
1 cup Hawaiian cane sugar
2 eggs
1 teaspoon lemon juice

2 teaspoon baking powder
1/2 teaspoon baking soda
1/2 cup shortening (butter or margarine)
1 cup mashed bananas
1 cup macadamia nuts, chopped

Sift dry ingredients together. Add shortening, eggs, and 1/2 cup bananas. Stir to combine ingredients, then beat 2 minutes at medium speed with electric mixer. Add remaining bananas and lemon juice. Beat 2 more minutes. Fold in 3/4 cup macadamia nuts. Pour into a greased, lined loaf pan (8 1/2 x 1/2). Sprinkle remaining 1/4 cup macadamia nuts over top of batter. Bake in moderate oven at 350º for 1 hour. Makes one loaf.

LAMB CHOPS WITH PAPAYA SALSA

6 3-1/2 ounce lamb sirloin chops
1/2 teaspoon salt
1 tablespoon cracked black pepper

3 cloves garlic, puréed
2 teaspoons oil

Rub both sides of chops with garlic. Season with salt. Press black pepper into chops on both sides and set aside. Coat oil in skillet and place over moderately high heat for 1 1/2 minutes. Add chops to the skillet and brown them, uncovered, for 2 minutes on each side. Transfer to platter, spoon salsa around chops, garnish with mint or watercress and serve immediately.

PAPAYA SALSA

1 cup ripe papaya, peeled, seeded and diced
1/4 cup roasted red bell pepper, peeled, seeded and diced
2 tablespoons white round onion, finely chopped
1 tablespoon mint leaves, cut in thin slivers
1 tablespoon cilantro leaves, chopped
1/2 teaspoon ground cumin
1/4 teaspoon curry powder

1/4 teaspoon salt or to taste
1 1/2 teaspoon lime juice

Mix all ingredients together. Allow to stand 1 hour before serving.

PEAR CRISP
Donnie Walsh, General Manager
Indiana Pacers

7 pears (peeled and sliced)
1 stick of butter or margarine (softened)
1 cup sugar
1 cup flour
cinnamon/sugar mixture

WASH peel and slice pears. Place in 9 x 12 glass baking dish. Combine butter and sugar, then add flour (mixture will be crumbly). Place butter, sugar, flour mixture on top of pears.

SPRINKLE with cinnamon/sugar mixture. Bake at 350° until brown or fruit sticks well. Serve with vanilla ice cream!

Other fresh fruit may be substituted for variety, e.g. cherries, peaches, etc.

OKLAHOMA BBQ BEEF KABOBS
David Walters
Governor, Oklahoma

1 cup water
1/2 cup soy sauce
1/4 cup brown sugar
1/4 cup lemon juice
1 small onion, sliced
1 garlic clove, minced
1 beef bouillon cube, crushed
3 pounds sirloin strips, cubed
20 cherry tomatoes
2 green peppers, cubed
1 pound mushroom caps
2 medium onions, cubed

Combine first 7 ingredients in large bowl with lid. Add meat and marinate in refrigerator for 24 hours. Stir occasionally. Alternate beef and vegetables on skewers. Grill over medium hot coals or broil in oven for about 15 minutes, turning frequently and basting with marinade. Serves 6 to 8.

MARINATED CHICKEN BREASTS

3 cups pineapple juice
3/4 cup soy sauce
1 cup sherry (dry)
1/2 cup red wine vinegar

2/3 cup sugar
1 1/2 teaspoons garlic powder
1 1/2 teaspoons powdered ginger
10-12 boned chicken breasts

Mix all ingredients, reserving 1 cup of marinade, and pour over chicken breasts. Marinate at least 12 hours or overnight. Cook over charcoal grill. Serve with wild rice that has been prepared with reserved marinade and 1 cup of fresh mushrooms.

CHOCOLATE CHIP COOKIES

2 1/4 cups all-purpose flour
1 teaspoon salt
3/4 cup sugar
1 teaspoon vanilla
2 cups chocolate chips

1 teaspoon baking soda
1 cup Butter Flavor Crisco
3/4 cup brown sugar
2 eggs
1 cup chopped nuts (optional)

Cream shortening and eggs until fluffy. Add sugars and vanilla. Combine flour, salt and baking soda. Gradually add to egg and shortening mixture. Stir in chocolate chips and nuts. Drop by teaspoonful onto ungreased cookie sheet. Bake at 375° for 9-11 minutes. Makes 5 dozen.

CHICKEN & DUMPLINGS
Dionne Warwick
Singer

Dionne calls this: "...one of my favorite recipes. I especially like it the way that my mother prepares it."

1 4-1/2 to 5 pound stewing chicken, cut up
3 celery tops
1 medium onion studded with 3 whole cloves
1 carrot sliced
2 bay leaves
1 tablespoon salt
3 cups hot water

In 8-quart sauce pot over high heat, heat to boiling chicken, neck and giblets, and remaining ingredients; reduce heat. Cover; simmer 2 to 2 1/2 hours. Discard onion, celery and bay leaves.

Dumplings

In large bowl with fork, stir 1 1/3 cups all-purpose flour, 2 teaspoons double-acting baking powder, 1 teaspoon chopped parsley and 1/2 teaspoon salt until mixed.

In cup, combine 2/3 cup milk with 2 tablespoons salad oil; slowly stir into flour until soft dough forms. Drop by heaping tablespoons onto chicken.

Cook uncovered 10 minutes; cover and cook 10 minutes more. With slotted spoon, remove dumplings. Spoon chicken into serving dish: top with dumplings.

"I hope that you enjoy this recipe as much as my family does."

VEAL SCALLOPINE WITH CHEESE AND MADEIRA SAUCE
Lowell P. Weicker, Jr., Governor
Connecticut

2 pounds veal scallopine (sliced thin and lightly breaded)
1/2 cup butter
3 tablespoons Madeira
1 tablespoon flour
1/2 cup milk
1 bouillon cube
1/4 teaspoon nutmeg
freshly ground black pepper
1/2 pound Gruyere or Ementhaler cheese, grated
1 cup water

Heat 6 tablespoons of butter in a skillet over medium heat, add veal and cook until browned on both sides. **(Do not over cook!)** Remove veal to a plate.

Add Madeira to the skillet and cook for a few seconds, scrapping particles on the bottom. Set skillet aside.

To make sauce

Bring water and milk to a boil in a saucepan and dissolve the bouillon cube in the mixture. In another small saucepan, melt remaining 2 tablespoons butter, add flour, and stir with a wire whisk until blended. Add water-milk mixture to this at once, stirring continuously until thickened, well blended, and smooth. Add nutmeg and season with pepper.

Arrange veal in a single layer in a shallow baking dish. Pour sauce over veal and top with grated cheese.

Dish can be refrigerated at this point for several hours. Before serving, heat oven to 425° and heat veal until cheese melts and turns brown, about 20 minutes.

"EGGS A LA BILL"
Bill Weld
Governor, Massachusetts

2 eggs
2 tablespoons of milk
salt to taste
pepper to taste
2 tablespoons of Orange Juice!
1 tablespoon of butter or margarine

IN a medium bowl, add all of the ingredients and mix well. Heat a skillet, melt the butter, and pour in the eggs. With a fork, scramble the eggs until well cooked. When eggs are done, serve with two pieces of toast and some sausages or bacon.

Serves 1

Enjoy!

CRUNCHY PIE
Betty White
Actress - Animal Lover

Beat three (3) egg whites until stiff
Add 1 teaspoon baking powder
Fold in 1 <u>scant</u> cup granulated sugar
Fold in eleven (11) single graham crackers (crushed)
Fold in 1 cup chopped walnuts

*P*ut in greased pie plate and bake in 350º oven for one-half hour.

*L*et cool and top with whipped cream or ice cream.

COTTAGE CHEESE SALAD
Vanna White
TV Personality

1 (3 ounces) box jello (I use lime flavored)

1 (32 ounces) plain cottage cheese

1 (8 ounces) can crushed pineapple (in it's own juice)

1 (8 ounces) container Cool Whip Whipped Topping   (regular or lite)

*"You can also add chopped walnuts
or pecans if desired."*

In a bowl put cottage cheese and then pour dry jello mix right from the box over it. Mix well. Drain pineapple, then add pineapple to mixture.

Fold in Cool Whip.   *Vanna*

Refrigerate until ready to serve.

WHOLE WHEAT PANCAKES
John Williams, Musician and Conductor
Boston Symphony Orchestra

"Serves the two of us with one left-over!"

Beat *together*

1 egg
1 cup non-fat plain yogurt
1 tablespoon butter
1 tablespoon maple syrup
1 teaspoon vanilla

Add & whisk *until just blended*

1 cup whole wheat pastry flour
1 teaspoon baking powder
3/4 teaspoon salt - or less
1/2 teaspoon baking soda
nutmeg - optional

Add non-fat milk to achieve desired consistency.

Use *a non-stick griddle if possible.*

MARYLAND CRAB CAKES
Montel Williams
Talk Show Host

1 pound fresh crab meat, shelled and cleaned
20 no - or low-salt saltine crackers, crushed fine
crushed red-pepper flakes to taste
1 ½ tablespoon Old Bay Seasoning
2 tablespoons dried parsley, crushed
½ cup mayonnaise
1 tablespoon Worcestershire sauce
1 large egg
3 shakes Tabasco sauce
1 teaspoon dry mustard or 1 tablespoon prepared dijon mustard
vegetable oil for frying

In a large bowl, combine crab meat, crackers, red-pepper flakes, Old Bay, and parsley.

In separate bowl, mix mayonnaise, Worcestershire, egg, Tabasco, and mustard. Combine with crab mixture and form into patties, using about 3 tablespoons for each.

In large skillet heat enough vegetable oil to cover patties at least halfway. When oil is sizzling, add patties and fry 3 minutes on each side, or until golden-brown. Drain. Serves 4.

BARBECUE CHICKEN
Pete Wilson
Governor, California

4-6 skinless chicken breasts

Paul Newman's's Italian Salad Dressing

dijon mustard

Lawrey's Seasoning Salt

pepper

First baste chicken on all sides with mustard, then baste with salad dressing, seasoned with salt and pepper. Place chicken on grill and sear until meat turns from pink to white on both sides. Baste once again with same ingredients and continue grilling until meat is done.

Enjoy!

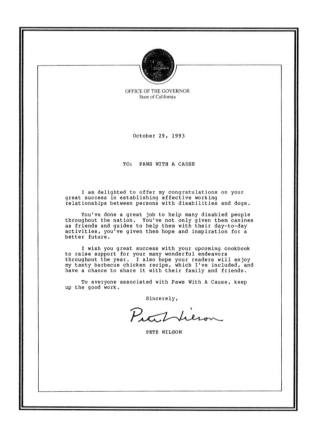

OFFICE OF THE GOVERNOR
State of California

October 29, 1993

TO: PAWS WITH A CAUSE

I am delighted to offer my congratulations on your great success in establishing effective working relationships between persons with disabilities and dogs.

You've done a great job to help many disabled people throughout the nation. You've not only given them canines as friends and guides to help them with their day-to-day activities, you've given them hope and inspiration for a better future.

I wish you great success with your upcoming cookbook to raise support for your many wonderful endeavors throughout the year. I also hope your readers will enjoy my tasty barbecue chicken recipe, which I've included, and have a chance to share it with their family and friends.

To everyone associated with Paws With A Cause, keep up the good work.

Sincerely,

PETE WILSON

TOMATO BEEF RECIPE
Senator and Mrs. Harris Wofford
U. S. Senate - Pennsylvania

*"May be partially prepared ahead,
or may be cooked at the table."*

2-3 pounds sirloin, top round or flank steak
1/2 pound fresh mushrooms
1 large onion (or 2 small)
1 large green pepper (or 2 small)
4 tomatoes
1 1/2 teaspoons cornstarch
2 tablespoons sherry
1/2 cup water
2 1/2 tablespoons soy sauce*
2 tablespoons sugar

Slice steak into strips 2 inches long and 1 inch thick, cutting across the grain. Slice the mushrooms. Cut the tomatoes, green pepper, and onion into large chunks.

In hot skillet (390° in electric skillet), add tablespoon oil and sauté mushrooms. When the mushrooms are partially cooked, add the onions, and cook these quickly. Push both of these to the side of the pan and add the slices of steak and two pieces of tomato. Mash tomato to give a touch of tomato flavor to the sauce.

Brown the steak quickly and sprinkle on the sugar, sherry, and soy. Add green peppers and remaining tomatoes. Make a paste of cornstarch and water and add that to the pan. Cook three more minutes and serve over hot rice.

*If Chinese shoyu sauce is used, decrease the shoyu to 2 tablespoons and increase the sugar to 2 1/2 tablespoons.

September 12, 1994

Dear Friends,

Since its beginning in November of 1979, we have seen over 900 PAWS® Teams come together ... that's 900 people and 900 dogs ... people gaining independence and dogs gaining purpose.   We have been blessed with the opportunity to witness our growth and the many miracles that have accompanied it. Countless moments of joy comc to mind.

The most valuable gift you can give us is your partnership. It is the one thing that best describes all that we strive to accomplish. PAWS® is thankful for the roles you have all played in establishing the finest and largest program for Hearing and Service Dogs in the country.

Welcome to a partnership of caring, kindness and independence!

Sincerely,

Mike
Candye

Mike and Candye Sapp

Here's one from the Sapp Kitchen

Delicious Cookies

1 cup miniature marshmallows
1 cup peanuts (salted)
1 cup rice crispies
12 ounces white chocolate
(white chocolate stars work best!)
2 tablespoons peanut butter

Mix dry ingredients. Melt chocolate and peanut butter in double boiler. or Microwave covered until mixture is soft (careful not to burn) - approximately 1 1/2 to 2 minutes. Pour over rice crispies mixture. Mix well. Spoon out onto wax paper and it makes approximately 2 to 2 1/2 dozen cookies, depending on how big a spoon you use. Or press in 9 inch square pan and cut to serve. Feel free to add a little extra of whatever you like best!

INDEX OF PARTICIPANTS

WORLD LEADERS

SPORTS FIGURES

ADDITIONAL - V.I.P's

INDEX OF RECIPES

MAIN COURSE

DESSERTS & SWEETS

MISCELLANEOUS

MEASUREMENTS

a pinch	⅛ teaspoon or less
3 teaspoons	1 tablespoon
4 tablespoons	¼ cup
8 tablespoons	½ cup
12 tablespoons	¾ cup
16 tablespoons	1 cup
2 cups	1 pint
4 cups	1 quart
4 quarts	1 gallon
8 quarts	1 peck
4 pecks	1 bushel
16 ounces	1 pound
32 ounces	1 quart
8 ounces liquid	1 cup
1 ounce liquid	2 tablespoons
1 stick of butter or margarine	8 tablespoons
2 sticks of butter or margarine	1 cup
4 sticks of butter or margarine	1 pound
2 cups of granulated sugar	1 pound
3 ½ cups of all purpose flour	1 pound

ABBREVIATIONS

c.	cup
tsp	teaspoon
tbsp	tablespoon
pkg	package
lb	pound
sq	square
pt	pint
qt	quart
gal	gallon

Metric Conversion Chart

Weight

To change	to	Multiply by
ounces	grams	30.0
pounds	kilograms	0.45
g rams	ounces	0.035
kilograms	pounds	2.2

Volume

To change	to	Multiply by
teaspoons	milliliters	5.0
tablespoons	milliliters	15.0
fluid ounces	milliliters	30.0
cups	liters	0.24
pints	liters	0.47
quarts	liters	0.95
gallons	liters	3.8
milliliters	fluid ounces	0.03
llters	pints	2.1
liters	quarts	1.06
liters	gallons	0.26

To Convert
FARHRENHEIT into CENTIGRADE

Example

‣	Subtract 32	100ºC x 9	= 900º
‣	Multiply by 5	900º ÷ 5	= 180º
‣	Divide by 9	180º + 32	= 212º

To convert Centigrade into Farhrenheit go into reverse:

- ‣ Multiply by 9
- ‣ Divide by 5
- ‣ Add 32

Moderate Oven

- ‣ 350º Farhrenheit = 177º Centigrade

Toastin' the Dogs™
Recipes of the Famous and Distinguished

NOTES

Toastin' the Dogs™
Recipes of the Famous and Distinguished

NOTES

Toastin' the Dogs™
Recipes of the Famous and Distinguished

NOTES

Toastin' the Dogs™
Recipes of the Famous and Distinguished

NOTES

Toastin' the Dogs™
Recipes of the Famous and Distinguished

NOTES

Toastin' the Dogs™
Recipes of the Famous and Distinguished

NOTES

Toastin' the Dogs™
Recipes of the Famous and Distinguished

ORDER FORM

If you would like to purchase additional copies of *Toastin' the Dogs*™ and you can't find it at your local bookstore, you can order it by mailing a completed copy of this form with a check or money order to:

Paws With A Cause®
1235 100th Street SE
Byron Center, Michigan   49315

Credit Card Phone Orders can be made by calling 1-800-253-PAWS between 9:30 am and 4 pm (EST) Monday through Friday. You can fax your order to us at (616) 698-2988.

Here's my order for *Toastin' the Dogs*™.

Quantity _____ $16.95   = $_____

Add your State Sales Tax   = $_____

Shipping Charge ($2.50 per book)   = $_____

Total Amount Enclosed   = $_____

SHIP ORDER TO:

Name:_____

Address:_____

City:_____State_____Zip_____

Daytime Phone:_____

Credit Card Orders (accepted at Headquarters only)
☐ Visa   ☐ MasterCard   ☐ American Express

Expiration Date: _____
Card Number: _____
Cardholders Name: _____

Signature: _____

Toastin' the Dogs™
Recipes of the Famous and Distinguished

ORDER FORM

If you would like to purchase additional copies of *Toastin' the Dogs*™ and you can't find it at your local bookstore, you can order it by mailing a completed copy of this form with a check or money order to:

Paws With A Cause®
1235 100th Street SE
Byron Center, Michigan   49315

Credit Card Phone Orders can be made by calling 1-800-253-PAWS between 9:30 am and 4 pm (EST) Monday through Friday. You can fax your order to us at (616) 698-2988.

Here's my order for *Toastin' the Dogs*™.

Quantity _____ $16.95   = $_____

Add your State Sales Tax   = $_____

Shipping Charge ($2.50 per book)   = $_____

Total Amount Enclosed   = $_____

SHIP ORDER TO:

Name:_____

Address:_____

City:_____State_____Zip_____

Daytime Phone:_____

Credit Card Orders (accepted at Headquarters only)
☐ Visa   ☐ MasterCard   ☐ American Express

Expiration Date: _____
Card Number: _____
Cardholders Name: _____

Signature: _____

Toastin' the Dogs™
Recipes of the Famous and Distinguished

ORDER FORM

If you would like to purchase additional copies of *Toastin' the Dogs*™ and you can't find it at your local bookstore, you can order it by mailing a completed copy of this form with a check or money order to:

Paws With A Cause®
1235 100th Street SE
Byron Center, Michigan   49315

Credit Card Phone Orders can be made by calling 1-800-253-PAWS between 9:30 am and 4 pm (EST) Monday through Friday. You can fax your order to us at (616) 698-2988.

Here's my order for *Toastin' the Dogs*™.

Quantity _____ $16.95   = $_____

Add your State Sales Tax   = $_____

Shipping Charge ($2.50 per book)   = $_____

Total Amount Enclosed   = $_____

SHIP ORDER TO:

Name:_____

Address:_____

City:_____State_____Zip_____

Daytime Phone:_____

Credit Card Orders (accepted at Headquarters only)
☐ Visa   ☐ MasterCard   ☐ American Express

Expiration Date: _____
Card Number: _____
Cardholders Name: _____

Signature: _____